Also by Sophie Hannah from Carcanet Press

The Hero and the Girl Next Door
Hotels Like Houses
Leaving and Leaving You
First of the Last Chances
Pessimism for Beginners

SOPHIE HANNAH

Marrying the Ugly Millionaire
New and Collected Poems

CARCANET

First published in Great Britain in 2015 by
Carcanet Press Limited
Alliance House
Cross Street
Manchester M2 7AQ

www.carcanet.co.uk

We welcome your comments on our publications
Write to us at info@carcanet.co.uk

A CIP catalogue record for this book is available from the British Library

ISBN
978 1 78410 025 4 pb
978 1 78410 026 1 hb

The publisher acknowledges financial assistance from Arts Council England

Typeset by XL Publishing Services, Exmouth
Printed and bound in England by SRP Ltd, Exeter

for Dan, Phoebe, Guy and Brewster, with love

Contents

New Poems

From *Early Bird Blues*

From *Second Helping of Your Heart*

The Hero and the Girl Next Door

Hotels Like Houses

Leaving and Leaving You

Pessimism for Beginners

I

New Poems

Unbalanced

'Cambridge has a very unbalanced demographic – there's an unnaturally high concentration of intelligent people.'

There is a lot that's wrong with Cambridge, yes:
Houses are too expensive and too thin,
The Clifton Leisure Park is nothing less
Than standing proof that a grave mortal sin
Can be committed by a multiscreen
Cinema allied with a Travelodge.
A Cambridge street is no idyllic scene:
Often, on King's Parade, I have to dodge
Tourists who wish to bash me in the face
With their huge cameras. I contain my rage,
Remind myself that I don't own the place –
I must play nice and share my Chronophage,
And thank my stars. Hemmed in by Hills Road traffic,
I savour the unbalanced demographic.

The Whole World Knows

I wasn't going to say this, but I will:
The Bourne Identity is on TV.
Hills Road is flat and nowhere near a hill.
I often wish that Woodlands Surgery
Would hire Greg House and his long-suffering team:
Foreman, Chase, Cuddy, Cameron, Wilson too.
Don't tell me it's an unrealistic dream.
They don't exist, no, but the actors do
So something could be done, presumably
(Though I've heard Chase and Cameron make a bid
For freedom at the end of Season 3).
I wasn't going to say that but I did.

I wasn't going to say this but I will.
We hear that line and know what to expect:
Words that will shrivel us and drive a chill
Through our warm hearts. *Why bother to protect*
Someone as reckless/ignorant/deranged
As your grim self? You've asked for trouble now.
You started this. I'd tactfully arranged
To swallow my disgust, avoid a row,
Spare your frail ego all my killer blows,
But since your disrespect is off the grid
You can take this: you're scum. The whole world knows.
I wasn't going to say that but I did.

The introduction's part of the attack:
Protection offered only when withdrawn.
Ought I to want the lesser insult back?
Oh, for our hey-day, when you hid your scorn!
Anyway, I intend to steal your line,
Use it to herald harmless observations,
Hopes, sometimes dreams. I'm turning it benign.
I adore living close to railway stations!
Less than five minutes' walk to catch the train!
I wasn't going to say this but I will,

Because I feel like sharing an inane
Fact with a friend. Reader, you fit the bill.
My favourite painting cost me forty quid!
Here's looking at spontaneous outbursts, kid.
I wasn't going to say that, but I did.

Hodder Sales Conference

for Robyn Young, unsurprisingly

I stayed up far too late last night
With Robyn Young, again.
This morning, I don't feel quite right.
We stayed up drinking all last night.
There we both were at dawn's first light
Discussing love and men.
I stayed up far too late last night
With Robyn Young, again.

You'd think we had no books to write.
All those who left at ten
Woke up this morning feeling bright.
Perhaps they'd like our books to write.
My brain feels like it's had a fight.
Now for some Nurofen.
We stayed up drinking all last night.
Mustn't do that again.

Gratitude

Thank you so much for sending back my scarf!

Oh, right. You're welcome. Er…you couldn't just go and say thank you to my wife, could you? She was a bit upset that you didn't send a card at the time.

(To wife) Thank you so much for sending back my scarf! I meant to write and thank you, but I probably forgot…

Yes. You did.

I left my scarf behind. You sent it on.
I meant to buy and send a Thank You card
But I forgot, and soon the year was gone
And the year after that. My life was hard

In those two years, not in a tragic sense –
Not trapped, like Chilean miners, underground
Nor starved behind a grim high-voltage fence –
Hard in an arty way: the endless round

Of thriller panels, signings, foreign tours,
Mixed in with children's homework, costumes, lice.
I'll show you my list if you'll show me yours.
Mine's longer. Take your pick: I'm either nice

And ludicrously busy, or a bitch
Who takes good deeds for granted, doesn't care.
Here, have the stupid scarf back. Stitch by stitch,
Unpick, unpick. My neck prefers cold air.

The Little Cushion and the Empty Chair

I'm paying you to listen and I'm paying you to care.
I don't have many problems. Well, let's say I have my share.
Before we start this therapy, I think it would be fair
To warn you of my limits. You will need to be aware:
I cannot beat a cushion or accuse an empty chair.

The cushion's looking innocent. It's recently been plumped.
I'm having plaguing visions of it battered, torn and slumped.
Yes, it's inanimate and therefore happy to be thumped.
I'm sure it has been, many times – by the depressed, the dumped,
The discombobulated. I'll abstain. Say if you're stumped –

I'll understand. I'm stumped myself. I ought to know the drill.
It's therapy. Why won't my mind co-operate and fill
Your empty chair with someone who ideally fits the bill?
It's not that I don't want to; I entirely lack the skill.
I can't berate a chair. I never could. I never will.

I also can't write letters that I'm never going to send.
(Might as well tell you now – you're going to find out in the end.)
Lies I do well, but I cannot cathartically pretend,
Which has a happy side effect that I did not intend:
The chair thinks I'm all right. The little cushion is my friend.

The Dalai Lama on Twitter

We do as much harm to ourselves and to others when we take offence
as when we give offence.

I am following the Dalai Lama on Twitter
But the Dalai Lama is not yet following me.
That's fine. Things are as they are. I do not feel bitter.
Enlightenment is his thing. Reciprocity?
Not so much. He is a spiritual big-hitter
And I write detective novels. It's easy to see
Why I'm following the Dalai Lama on Twitter
And the Dalai Lama is not yet following me.

He doesn't know how often I pick up litter,
How many signed books I have given away for free,
Not to Russell Brand, Wayne Rooney or Gary Glitter
But as raffle prizes for this or that charity,
And since I would hate to think of myself as a quitter –
Because I, at least, know it isn't all about me –
I am following the Dalai Lama on Twitter
Even though he is self-absorbed to the nth degree.

You'd think a sage of his rank would know about karma,
About courtesy, and the decent thing to do.
Oh, follow me, follow me, follow me, Dalai Lama!
I'm an expert on *House MD* and crime fiction too.
I wouldn't DM you outlandish theories of Dharma
Or make you retweet my latest good review.
I am following, on Twitter, the Dalai Lama
But the Dalai Lama has not thought to follow me too.

(PS – Eckhart Tolle, this also applies to you.)

I Cannot In All Conscience Share a Platform
With The Train

I cannot in all conscience share a platform with the train.
It's always overheated and refuses to explain.
Instead it scuttles off, as cowards do, to Audley End.
Condemn and shun the train or I'll no longer be your friend.

It isn't just the heat. You heard the buffet car admit
It has sold out of crisps. And that is not the worst of it.
The loos (the buffet's allies) smell of hamsters, and the bloke
Who checked our tickets laughed – no doubt at an offensive joke.

Don't tell me cars and planes pollute the air with noxious fumes.
Yes, the Titanic stashed the rich and poor in separate rooms.
Are you suggesting I'm to blame? Then why the veiled attack?
My point is that this train should have a better luggage rack –

One that would take my weight but not make stripe marks on
                                                        my bum.
Before I disembark, I challenge everyone to come
And check my reputation for that nonexistent stain.
I cannot in all conscience share a platform with the train.

The Storming

There are differences, one assumes,
between us and the people we know who storm out of rooms,

sometimes crying, but not every time;
sometimes muttering, sometimes an angry marching mime

is their exit mode. Where do they go,
all those people who storm out of rooms? Will we ever know?

Are there sandwiches there, and a flask
of hot tea? We won't find out if we never ask.

Once they've fled the provoking scene,
do they all get together somewhere? Do they reconvene

in a basement, an attic, a flat?
Do they also reserve the right to storm out of that,

and if so, do they take turns to storm
or link arms and desert en masse in a furious swarm,

leaving nobody in their wake?
Would there be any point in the storming, for nobody's sake?

There are differences, one fears,
between us and the people who storm out of rooms in tears,

as if, having ruined it all
in the snug, they imagine they'll be better off in the hall,

and that anyone left in a chair
automatically gets to be wrong and to blame and unfair,

unaware of how bad stormers feel,
and quite lacking in feelings themselves. That is part of the deal.

Notice how I don't leap to my feet,
how I nestle in cushions and curl myself into my seat.

Leave at once for the moral high ground.
I'll stay here by the fire, mocking storms and just lounging around.

The One Who Should Be Crying

What are you crying for?
I'm the one who should be crying.

What are you writing a poem called
The One Who Should Be Crying for?
I'm the one who should be writing a poem
called *Emotions Must Be Earned
And Exchanged, Like Vouchers, For Something Worth Having,*
                                                Like Rules.

What are you dreaming about me for?
I have never staged a show trial in a hall
while you signed your books in a cramped room next door.

I'm not responsible for what you dream about.
I've forced your authentic self into hiding? Prove it,
or this conversation ends here.

Multiple Warning Survivors Anonymous

Please don't warn me of things that won't happen,
Like: the man who just sold me some land
Might in fact have a vat
Of the plague in his hat
And a new black death minutely planned.

Please don't mention unlikely disasters
That you think I'd be wise to avoid:
Getting stalked in a tent,
Or inhaling cement…
Yes, my life could be swiftly destroyed

But it won't be, so no need to summon
Your great ally, the spectre of doom –
Babies, injured or dead!
Dearest friend, axe in head! –
While I'm safe, sitting still in a room.

I am sure I'll avoid strangulation
By a dangling invisible thread,
But my life's in bad shape
If I cannot escape
From these horrors you plant in my head.

Can I tell you what *I* think is likely?
And I hope this is not out of line:
Yes, there is a small chance
I'll be stabbed by Charles Dance
But I strongly suspect I'll be fine,

Or I would be, if only you'd zip it.
No, I won't wear a bullet-proof vest
When I go to Ikea.
Don't troll me with fear.
Here's a warning: just give it a rest

Or I'll certainly spend most of Sunday
Thinking you're an assiduous scourge –
Sure as peas grow in pods.
Please consider those odds
When you next feel the dread-warning urge.

If one day I am crushed by a hippo
Then my agent will give you a ring.
If you like you can mourn me,
But please, please – don't warn me.
Your warning's my only bad thing.

Two Poems about the Alternative Voting System (AV)

1) A LIMERICK

'Person X is my choice number one,
And my second choice…'
                              'Don't jump the gun!
Person X is still in. Wait, he's out and can't win.'

'So my second choice…'
                              'Sorry, we're done.'

2) A HAIKU

1,2. 1,2,3.
1,2,3,4. 1,2,3.
1,2. 1,2. 1.

A Christmas Truce

What would I like for Christmas?
A close friend wants to know.
Perfume? A clock? A spa day?
Some tickets for a show?

'I need ideas by Monday,'
She huffs, as if I'm not
Sufficiently respectful
Of her present-buying slot,

Which will expire by Tuesday,
Her harried tone implies.
Art books? Posh wine? New teapot?
Brainstorm! Prioritise!

What do I want for Christmas?
I want you not to ask.
I'd rather get no gifts at all
Than be assigned the task

Of emailing a wish list
(One I must first create)
To all my friends and family
Before a certain date.

Can I propose a Christmas truce
To make my dreams come true?
Create no work for me and I'll
Create no work for you.

I've got enough possessions –
Shoes, coats, a diamond ring –
I want not to be asked to do
A time-consuming thing.

Yes, that's a proper present –
Abstract, but no less real.
What do you mean it seems as if
I don't care how you feel?

ALL RIGHT! I'll have a teapot.
What? Then wrap it in a fleece.
Yes, I will ring to say it got here
Safely, in one piece.

Frumpy Secret

I have a frumpy secret,
Too stupid to withhold.
It's practical, it's legal,
And it must not be told.

I have been doing something
I'm not supposed to do,
So everyday, so humdrum,
You'd nod off if you knew.

It lacks the haggard glamour
That ought to go with sin.
It's almost as dramatic
As emptying the bin

And yet, for crazy reasons
That I cannot explain
Without offending someone,
I'm stuck with this insane

And uninspiring secret
I've no desire to keep.
No, really. No, you wouldn't.
I can't. Go back to sleep.

If You Were Standing Where His Shadow Fell

The tyrant's favourite chocolates are Maltesers.
We roll them at his toes, surround his feet.
They drop through grates; we pluck them out with tweezers.
He sulks. They are too round and brown and sweet.

The tyrant thinks a soppy armadillo
would make an ideal pet: tough shell, limp heart.
He keeps a doodle underneath his pillow.
The rest is down to us. He's done his part;

we have to find it, buy it, love it, feed it,
teach it that we're its slaves, ignore the swell
of indignation, since we'll never need it.
If you were standing where his shadow fell

you'd willingly succumb to his distortions.
You'd contemplate revenge, then rule it out.
He's living what he's earned, in hefty portions:
each day, each year. Oh, he is in no doubt

that we confide in lamps, bond with umbrellas,
in preference to him. This is our fault,
or so he thinks, confining us to cellars.
He'll remain unaware. Exalt! Exalt

when he releases you; embrace the terror
of his renewed attack before too long.
For your sake and for his, don't make the error
of showing him he's all the bad and wrong.

Frequently Asked Questions

1. Is the lying the point, or are the disappearances the point?

2. Do you worry about being found out?

3. Or do you have an enormous trust fund, so it doesn't really matter?

4. Why don't you tell everyone the same story?

5. Or would that be as tedious as telling the truth?

6. If you found out that I'd started lying to you, would you mind?

7. Do you secretly want to get caught?

8. Would you consider making an exception for books? Never lie about which ones you like or dislike? Never say you've read ones that you haven't?

9. Is it weird that if you answered 'yes' to question 8, I'd forgive you the rest?

10. Do you know that I know?

11. What's your email password? I won't use it, I promise. I'm only asking because Steven Spielberg said he'd never play badminton with me again if I didn't.

Growing Up Fast

Children grow up so madly fast.
My daughter, not yet eight,
Wants to know when a boyfriend will
Invite her on a date.

I'm all in favour of the trend.
At this rate, when she's ten
She will discover herbal tea
And *Monarch of the Glen*

And snuggly early nights with books.
Her drug-fuelled nightclub phase
Will be behind her (finished in
A record seven days,

Containing one 'I hate you', one
'God, that is *so* unfair'.)
By twelve, she'll love my killjoy streak
Because it proves I care,

By thirteen she'll have realised
She must suspect and doubt
Everything I have ever said.
At fourteen, she'll move out,

Find an alternative world view,
Forgive the gaping flaw
In mine for what it put her through,
And then she'll be mature.

Secondary Gain

If I have lost the sun, then I will need to keep the moon.
It's in the sky for now, but I'll collect it some time soon.
The universe has set to work without consulting me.
I will not let what can't be changed become my enemy –

That's because I'm a person who's determined to succeed.
I'll never say in public that I strongly disagreed,
Or that I fear the universe is a deranged buffoon,
And in return the universe will hand me down the moon.

I've given this some thought: the moon may still stay up all night.
It may continue to be round, high above ground, and white.
It must not be more like the sun than like a friend of mine.
It must decide that everything about me suits it fine.

When people try to tell me it's a crazy thing I've done,
I plan to turn on them and scream, 'All right, then – where's the sun?'
I'm proud to be the fool who'll never make the moon lie flat.
Also, I'm not the biggest fool. The universe is that.

Moderation

All of the things you never heard,
Things that I wish I'd said,
Can be reduced to just one word
That didn't leave my head

But sits, as if afraid to try,
On an embargoed shelf
Of vital messages that I
Sent only to myself

So I could stamp them unexpressed
And file them out of sight
In order that they pass the test
Of proving I'm polite,

That I can stand before a crowd
And still remain unseen
And speak a list of clues out loud –
Not half of what I mean –

That will be half misunderstood,
That listeners will recall
As safe, in that they did no good
For anyone at all.

Crowd Pleaser

'Are you here for the Milne Craig event?'
Asked the girl on reception last night,
So I made a vague noise of assent
Since I thought she'd be pleased to be right,

Though this made things quite tricky, because
I was now set to gatecrash a do
At which no one would know who I was,
Populated by no one I knew.

The receptionist saw my perplexed
And embarrassed expression, and said
Just the words that I hoped she'd say next:
'Or are you for the book thing instead?'

'Yes, the book thing.' I beamed. 'Clever you.'
She was right once again. All was fine
And I added myself to the queue
For the bash that was rightfully mine,

And I worried about my bizarre,
Decades-old and irrational fear
Of explaining how I think things are,
When some people might not want to hear,

When it might cause a frown or a stir
If my words or my views are too strong.
Someone tell me, so I can concur:
Sometimes I'm right, and others are wrong.

New Leaf

The leaf, before it hit the ground,
Begged me to axe the tree.
The leaf is in the compost mound
So now it's up to me.

The smoke, before it thinned in air,
Asked me to quell the fire.
That smoke is now not anywhere
To see the flames rise higher.

The tear, before it rolls, requests
The losing of the eye.
But if I do as it suggests
How will I ever cry,

Or see a leaf or leaping flame
Before it disappears,
Before one day takes all the blame
For endless ends of years?

Let's

Let's steal a clapped-out camper van
And push it to the edge
Of occupied Afghanistan.
Let's perch it on a ledge
Of sinking sand, and test how fast
Its punctured wheels will spin.
Whoever's lung collapses last
Must lift the van to win.

Let's roast the carcass of a beast
In sweat and single malt,
Subject whoever eats the least
To a prolonged assault,
Blindfolded, beer cans in the face;
Let's scale the sharpest rock
Straight from a polar ice floe race,
In hypothermic shock.

Is it high-risk and ill-thought-out?
Will victory equal pain?
Will all involved be plagued by doubt
Unless they are insane,
And will this be dismissed as grounds
To stop and think again?
I only ask because it sounds
Like a plan made by men.

Party Wall

I'm sorry if my voice shattered your peace.
As quietly as I could, since it was midnight,
I tiptoed to the phone and rang
the council's out-of-hours noise nuisance number.

I honestly didn't think you'd be disturbed.
Bohemian Rhapsody was playing
loudly, and at least ten drunks
(or however many guests you have tonight)
were shouting out the lyrics, while I spoke
briefly to someone from Environmental Health.

If I'd known my thanking her
for telling me that a noise abatement order
can be served on you, and that if you don't change
your ways, the next step will be confiscation
of your speakers and amps, and after that, prosecution –

if I'd known my saying, 'Thanks, that's good to hear'
would interrupt your enjoyment
of the throbbing bass lines of one floorboard-shaking
nostalgic hit after another,
of course I'd have waited till morning.

On the plus side, for you:
one, I've just hung up, and two,
cheerful anticipation makes no sound.
All you will hear is all I can hear for the rest of the night:
Madonna's *Cherish*, the Spice Girls' *Wannabe*, and my silence
as I lie in bed, picture you in the dock, and grin.

Injustice

Traffic police take no account
(In licence points, in fine amount)
Of the way love tends to erode
Our knowledge of the Highway Code.

A Besooned Thank-You

Thank you for letting me down so quickly.
It could have dragged on for a year or more.
At my age, one disappointing weekend –
as hard to forget as it is to endure –
is not a Top Ten or Top Twenty disaster,
so thank you for letting me down so much faster

than other men do. Did you know I was stressing?
I mentioned work deadlines and that they were tight.
This swift disillusionment's rather a blessing –
you won't even take up another whole night.
My keenness went into overdrive
between junction 12 of the M25

and junction 18. Then the following morning
you started dismantling all my hopes:
rinsing them down like trowels in the boot room
to toss in a cupboard with frayed skipping ropes,
torn gardening gloves, old shoes that have been
endlessly worn and a bugger to clean.

But thank you for letting me down so promptly,
for timing the on and the off of your charm
so precisely. Perhaps you too have a schedule
to keep to? Perhaps you set your alarm.
Now, please can you fuck off to Mars or the moon?
Thank you for letting me down so soon.

Not Miss Havisham

I assume you're short of women to undress with,
Or you're daft as only clever men can be.
When you brainstormed hearts to hoax and minds to mess with,
Why on God's green planet did you plump for me?

Did you want to end up in a nasty poem?
Will you benefit from this publicity?
Shall I say, 'Yes, it's about X – do you know him?'
If I did, would you be chuffed as chuffed can be?

Not Miss Havisham, but also not a doormat;
Do you know that I write novels, not just verse?
Would you like your dressing-down to be dual format?
You're unusual, if so – also perverse,

And not special, just another one to lump in
With the duds. Still, we all make hideous mistakes.
Shall I point the way to something you might jump in?
(I assume you're short of cold, commodious lakes.)

Risk a Verse

May I please be excused from this *folie à deux*?
It was fun while it lasted, but now I'd prefer
To be focused on work, in my nightie by ten;
Walk the dog, have a swim – back to normal again.

What becomes of such *folies* when one party tires
And is suddenly not what the other requires?
I have wept. I have worshipped. I've broken the law.
I've been foolish and fooled, but I'm not any more,

So, please, how do I cancel, escape or postpone?
Can't you be a cute sociopath on your own?
All this languishing under the spell of a freak
Has unearthed a rebellious sensible streak

I did not know I had. Can we skip the next lie?
Let me darn some school cardies and make shepherd's pie.
Bonnie, Clyde, Louise, Thelma – how daft they all were!
May I please be released from this *folie à deux*?

From *Early Bird Blues*

Cooking Lessons

The pasta's in the cupboard, dear.
You'll find a saucepan on the shelf.
Get your pathetic arse in gear
And make the bloody tea yourself.

Useless

This love is a useless pursuit
From which no good can come.
Oh, how I wish I'd been astute
And listened to my mum.

Thoughts on a Tree

(as it might have been written by Robert Frost)

When I walk out alone at night to pubs,
Is it the moaning of the trees I hear,
The soft, subdued lament of leafy shrubs
That are outsiders from the world of beer?

For how unsociable, how sad they are,
These rooted things, fated to stand and watch
And know that they can never reach a bar
Themselves, that they will never taste a scotch.

And yet we are alike in many ways –
I tend to be an introvert when drunk,
Just as the tree, on harsh and snowy days,
Takes refuge in its sturdiness of trunk.

Oh tree, unable as you are to frolic,
At least you won't become an alcoholic.

The Floozy in the Jacuzzi

I admit that I have an ulterior motive
but it isn't what you think.
I'm beginning to bore myself.

Too much effort has gone into keeping my secrets.
In case they turn out to be lies, I don't tell them.
More interesting things are happening outside

which I can't be bothered to discuss.
All I care about is myself and, of course,
you, in the usual revolting way.

I could say you bring out the worst in me
but in fact no change has occurred.
I'm the same as I've always been –

the fraud, the floozy in the jacuzzi.
What keeps me going is the idea
that I am my only hope and yours.

Breaking Free

I cannot draw the likeness of an apple.
I cannot draw the likeness of a tree
Or sketch a naked human form. I grapple
With watercolours unsuccessfully.

I can't mix paint, or understand perspective.
My work looks flat – I can't do three dimensions.
Perhaps I need to alter my objective,
Make my own rules, break free from all conventions.

I offer you the contents of my bin.
A pile of household waste is on display
In my front room. Here's a banana skin,
Here an old sock. I call this piece "Decay".

Townie

You've brought your map, your hiking boots –
You suggest a country stroll.
I'm sorry – I prefer to stick
To main roads, on the whole.
I'm what you'd call a townie –
My enthusiasm drops
At the thought of a large expanse of green
With few (if any) shops.

I don't think we're compatible –
You hate the Arndale Centre.
You show no trace of interest
In the new shade of magenta
Lipstick from Number Seventeen
While I detest sheer drops
And the thought of a large expanse of green
With few (if any) shops.

Multiple Choice

You hate it if I cry or raise my voice
Or ever drop my customary tact.
As you're the boss, I'm giving you the choice –
Please tell me how you'd like me to react.

Should I (a) get used to being treated badly
Or (b) just smile and act like nothing's wrong?
Should I (c) love everything about you madly
Or (d) be glad you've stayed with me so long?

Should I (e) switch off my mind and start undressing
Or (f) fight back my feelings and be brave?
Should I (g) accept the fact that life's depressing
Or (h) kneel down and be your willing slave?

I'll leave it up to you. Just pick a letter.
If that one doesn't work, we'll try another.
Gradually life should start to get much better
For one of us at least, if not the other.

The Burden

I keep you fresh. You're in my dreams and thoughts
And suffering in both. Revenge is slow.
Awake, I plan to drag you through the courts.

My word against... The burden... yes, I know.
Asleep, my brick-red lipstick gleams as I
Bad-mouth you on The Oprah Winfrey Show.

It's funny, though – I never make you die.
My conscious and subconscious minds agree
That you should be allowed another try,

Another chance to make it up to me.
Awake, asleep, I'd drop all charges then,
Forget how bad you were if you would be

A little worse, or just the same again.

No Wonder

This love looks set to grow extremely tall.
I chart its weekly progress on the wall

the way my Mum made pencil marks above
my sister's head and mine. I've called it love

since it began, but now I have some proof –
infatuation stops before the roof

while love climbs bravely up to bash its head.
The bleeding starts. No wonder hearts are red.

From *Second Helping of Your Heart*

Ballade

You couldn't be described as poor
Although I've often heard you say
That you could do with slightly more
To see you through your working day.
Somebody ought to raise your pay,
Buy you a big, expensive car.
If life was fair in any way
You would be richer than you are.

You'd have two guards outside your door,
A maid to bring your breakfast tray,
A cleaner for the kitchen floor,
A cat to chase the mice away,
An indoor court, where you could play
Tennis all year, a private bar,
Endless supplies of Chardonnay –
You would be richer than you are.

Your dietician would ensure
Your meals were balanced, fresh, okay.
Your psychotherapist would cure
Your mind of pain, distress, dismay.
Your faithful staff would never stray;
You would be treated like a star.
No-one would dare to disobey.
You would be richer than you are.

Envoi

Meanwhile I try to help. I pray
At night and leave my door ajar.
Rent out your rooms – I'll let you stay.
You would be richer than you are.

Incompetence

Sawdust lover, with a head that's lighter
than your jacket, are you walking
to the walnut shop with lenses
on your feet?
A plastic bag rolled up inside your cardigan
and shopping on your head, you pause,
unravelling the laces
of your shoes,
and paddle to the starting line where salad bowls
dissolve. The sun and rain both trickle
down your nose. You keep them
in your socks.
A slice of lemon sheds a drop in silence.
You were absent with a crumpled tissue
in your ear, but it was not
your fault.

Something You Should Know

There's something you should know about this town.
Details would take too long, but here's the gist:
White envelopes are much preferred to brown.

Fawn-coloured ones are greeted with a frown.
Don't call me over-cautious. I insist,
There's something you should know about this town:

Although there is the odd, disruptive clown
Who'll send a beige one when he's really pissed,
White envelopes are much preferred to brown.

For deviants, the only way is down.
It does no good to be an anarchist.
There's something you should know about this town,

(For even you, a man of high renown,
Could be the target of an angry fist) –
White envelopes are much preferred to brown.

They'll lock you up. You'll wear a starched, white gown
Hospital style. What's more, you won't be missed.
There's something you should know about this town:
White envelopes are much preferred to brown.

The Lazy Student's Song

I sunbathe hard, ignoring Robert Frost
For fear the heat might be returned to sender.
Work is a battle I've already lost.
I'm a good sport. I gracefully surrender.

For fear the heat might be returned to sender
I shut my eyes and stretch out on the grass.
I'm a good sport. I gracefully surrender.
Who wants to take exams? Who wants to pass?

I shut my eyes and stretch out on the grass.
My head is filled with angry tutors' faces.
Who wants to take exams? Who wants to pass?
Only the stressed-out fools, the real sad cases.

My head is filled with angry tutors' faces.
I know I'm in the right. I won't back down.
Only the stressed-out fools, the real sad cases,
Care more about good grades than getting brown.

I know I'm in the right. I won't back down.
Hell hath no fury like a student tanned.
Care more about good grades than getting brown?
I try, but I will never understand.

Hell hath no fury like a student tanned.
Now I must melt my fury in the sun.
I try but I will never understand –
Surely the most important thing is fun?

Now I must melt my fury in the sun.
Work is a battle I've already lost –
Surely the most important thing is fun?
I sunbathe hard, ignoring Robert Frost.

The Twinkliness of Stars

Embarrassing for someone like myself,
A practised cynic, boasting many scars,
To pull a Mills and Boon book off the shelf
And comment on the twinkliness of stars.

Luckily I am in the house alone
With nobody to see this hard face soften.
I watch romantic films and try to groan
As usual, as noisily, as often.

Embarrassing to walk around in trances,
To be the sort of silly girl who looks
Self-satisfied, face glowing as she glances
At gold and diamond rings in Beaverbrooks.

I grew up doubting everything, so smart,
Only to find I now believe in Cupid.
I'm sure I've grown a pink and fluffy heart
Since I became phenomenally stupid.

Embarrassing. This week I bought no beer;
Instead, I spent my cash on lacy bras.
My dreams, which once contained a healthy fear,
Now focus on the twinkliness of stars.

The Pink Egg Dances

I have no visions
and take no chances
with small decisions.

The pink egg dances,
rocks in my palm,
retreats, advances

slowly. No harm
is done, not to me,
not now. I stay calm,

motionless, see
where the egg will roll.
It is both free

and in control.
It feels no pain.
It has no soul.

When I explain
I understand.
Long may it reign

in my flat hand.

The Sort of Film I Hate

Close-ups of windows. Other pointless shots.
Somebody screams – we never find out why.
Voices are low to make us listen hard.
Nobody says, 'If you pull that in my
Courtroom again I'll see that you're disbarred.'
Somebody somewhere's never heard of plots.

Plenty of symbols. Not a single joke.
The characters are moody and intense.
This scene has no connection to the last.
Nothing that happens makes a jot of sense.
It's hard to tell the present from the past.
Isn't it time somebody moved or spoke?

Cameramen have tried to be artistic,
Filming from overhead or from the side.
Fast-forwarding would help increase the pace.
Nothing is stated. Everything's implied.
The soundtrack is the only saving grace.
'Subtle,' the critics say, 'and realistic.'

Nightmare

The floor is thickly carpeted with hair.
Small lions swim around a bowl of roses;
I hold their plimsolls. No-one sees me there,
Perched just inside a mouth that never closes.

The toothless preacher wears green dungarees
And waves a wooden rod. His legs are scarred.
Grimly, he builds an edifice of cheese
With seven archways and a birthday card.

A spring has broken free beneath the sofa.
Shirts ask permission to retain one sleeve.
I offer you a limousine and chauffeur –
That is how much I wish that you would leave.

Mind the Gap

It's difficult to find your way around
In London. I was smart. I brought a map.
Now I am standing in the Underground;
A tinny voice is saying 'mind the gap.'

Is it referring to the gap between
The platform and the train (the naked line
Could kill you in a flash), or does it mean
The tens of years between your age and mine?

Is it an omen? Have I gone insane,
Taking these disembodied words to heart?
No, it will never work, but here's the train
And I get on. Maybe I'm not so smart.

Peculiar Praise

I'd rather have you insincere
If that's the way you've always been
Than have you honest as of now.
My fear
Is that the man I've seen
Will change somehow,
Move, and a new, clean man appear

Who looks so different from the old
That I will fail to recognise
His admirable qualities.
Truth told,
I don't object to lies
Which tread with ease
Over a fact whose bones are cold.

What first attracts me is the gloss
On anyone. Yours is so bright,
So total, that I know I'd feel
A loss
If it fell out of sight,
And for the real
Beneath I couldn't give a toss.

The Hero and the Girl Next Door

Soft Companion

He sat in the under-heated flat, alone,
Usefully passing time (he thought by choice),
Not missing anything, until the phone
Brought him the soft companion of your voice,

And then he looked around himself and saw
The scraps of clothing on the floor, in shreds,
And felt his keys hang heavy in the door.
He thought of powdered milk and single beds.

Unsure of him, you said, 'It's only me,'
Meaning not quite enough, but you were right:
Yours was the only face he hoped to see
And only you remembered him tonight.

Summary of a Western

We see a dusty desert scene and that's
The way the film begins. Some men in hats
Deliver gritty lines. They all wear braces.
They're cool and tough. They hate the darker races
Who paint peculiar stripes across their faces.

Goodies meet baddies, mostly in corrals.
Cowboys ignore or patronise their gals.
We see a gun twirl in a macho hand.
Who's killing whom we don't quite understand –
There's always some vague reference to the land.

Women in aprons have to be protected.
Stagecoaches fall. New sheriffs are elected.
The cast consists primarily of horses –
They gallop to the ending, which of course is
A happy one, where nobody divorces.

Symptoms

Although you have given me a stomach upset,
weak knees, a lurching heart, a fuzzy brain,
a high-pitched laugh, a monumental phone bill,
a feeling of unworthiness, sharp pain
when you are somewhere else, a guilty conscience,
a longing, and a dread of what's in store,
a pulse rate for the *Guinness Book of Records* –
life now is better than it was before.

Although you have given me a raging temper,
insomnia, a rising sense of panic,
a hopeless challenge, bouts of introspection,
raw, bitten nails, a voice that's strangely manic,
a selfish streak, a fear of isolation,
a silly smile, lips that are chapped and sore,
a running joke, a risk, an inspiration –
life now is better than it was before.

Although you have given me a premonition,
chattering teeth, a goal, a lot to lose,
a granted wish, mixed motives, superstitions,
hang-ups and headaches, fear of awful news,
a bubble in my throat, a dare to swallow,
a crack of light under a closing door,
the crude, fantastic prospect of forever –
life now is better than it was before.

The Affair

The lamp post bends his head. His face is red
above the frozen fringes of the street.
Dishevelled night is climbing into bed.
She strokes the waking clock, then steals the sheet.

Something disturbs the symmetry of hedges;
a recent scandal seeping through the grass.
The breathing curtains lose their heavy edges,
touched by the light that settles on the glass.

A small dog kicks the pavement into stretching.
The postbox mouth hangs open for receiving.
I almost hear a taxi driver fetching
your suitcase. Very soon you will be leaving.

Six Sonnets

WHEN I AM FAMOUS

When I am famous, in the years to come,
I know how keen you'll be to share the glory;
When journalists whip out a hefty sum
Before your nose, to make you sell our story,
You'll have no qualms. I, therefore, will expect
Full details of our sex life in *The Sun*.
I will not sue you, nor will I object
In any way – I'll treat it as good fun.
Make sure to give them all the dirty bits.
The truth gets dull – why not throw in some lies,
Some strange inventions? Say I've got three tits
Or four. Meanwhile, I've got a nice surprise
In store for you – I'll make you tremble yet:
I know about your flower-pressing set.

WRONG AGAIN

I did the right thing once (may God reward me);
Restrained myself. I took a moral stance.
Virtue, I found, was not my thing – it bored me
Rigid, and I would like another chance
To earn myself a wicked reputation
Equal to yours. I'll match you sin for sin.
Lies, promiscuity, inebriation –
It all sounds lovely. When can we begin?
I used to be afraid of rumours spreading.
You made my fear seem fussy, immature.
Here's my new motto, then: just change the bedding
And carry on exactly as before.
A single, happy night beneath your quilt
Is all I want. I'll risk post-coital guilt.

THE PHILANDERER'S ANSAPHONE MESSAGE

I'm not at home to take your call. Bad luck,
But leave your number and I'll be in touch.
You'll hear from me next time I want a fuck
(My love, my darling). Thank you very much.
Please leave your name – I'll add it to my list,
That way I won't forget. One does lose track…
But I can guarantee that when I'm pissed
I shall be keen to get you in the sack.
I knew this ansaphone would come in handy –
Voice after female voice I've got recorded.
I play the tape back when I'm feeling randy
And one by one my ladies are rewarded.
My system works supremely well, I've found.
Wait by the phone until your turn comes round.

A SHALLOW END

It's not a present. Call it a reward.
The pool is yours. I'll charge you for the water.
A shallow end, perhaps, you could afford.
I would like a cut-price coffin to bury my daughter.

They give you rice or chips with every meal.
Look, two cremations for the price of one!
A car drives past without a single wheel.
I would like a second-hand coffin to bury my son.

My ornaments were sad to see me go.
I must remind them that we still vote Labour.
Return the plum tomato that you owe.
I would like a hole in the garden to bury my neighbour.

But to go to Rome and not speak a word of Latin!
I would like a very cheap coffin to bury my cat in.

ONE-TRACK MIND

Why does she take unnecessary trips?
She lives just opposite a row of shops.
She went to Crewe to buy a bag of chips.
She went to Birmingham to buy lamb chops.

She has no time for aeroplanes or boats.
She cannot get enough of British Rail.
She went to Liverpool for Quaker Oats
Then Halifax to buy the *Daily Mail.*

She went to Chester for a pair of tights.
Every weekend she's up and down some track.
She went to York for twenty Marlboro Lights.
She went to Stalybridge and came straight back.

Once, on her way to Hull for cottage cheese,
She saw him. All he said was *Tickets, please.*

Whoever cleans your windows once a week,
Whoever stuffs your letters through the door,
Whoever you'd get in to fix a leak –
I resent all of these and plenty more.

Men on the bus and women in the street,
Religious nuts who ring your bell at dawn,
Any chiropodist who's touched your feet,
Canvassers, tramps, whoever mows your lawn,

Your colleagues, friends, acquaintances (both sexes),
People with whom you've shared a cigarette,
Your enemies, and, most of all, your exes,
Everyone you have ever seen or met,

Voices you might from time to time have heard,
The speaking clock. Jealous is not the word.

Before Sherratt & Hughes Became Waterstone's

Romantic entanglements often occur
In a pub or a railway station,
But being a writer I tend to prefer
A suitably bookish location.

I've never liked nightclubs, nor am I the sort
To go for a snog in the loos.
By far the most interesting place to cavort
Is the ground floor of Sherratt & Hughes.

I've seen a few customers looking dismayed,
Too British to voice their objection,
But how can I help it? I like to get laid
just in front of the poetry section.

Most people prefer a luxurious setting –
A Mediterranean cruise,
But to my mind, the place most conducive to petting
Is the ground floor of Sherratt & Hughes.

All it takes is one glimpse of a gold-lettered spine
On those lovingly organised shelves
And a human encounter seems almost divine –
Not just sex, but a merging of selves.

I have never been someone who strictly adheres
To what's proper – I do as I choose.
(I go down very well with the male cashiers
On the ground floor of Sherratt & Hughes.)

Two-Headed Dog Street

Walking down two-headed dog street on my
way to work is such an upsetting
experience that I prefer to stay at home.

I prefer to stay at home, but I
have trouble conveying this to my
boss, who is lucky enough to have never
needed to walk down two-headed dog street.

Two-headed dog street is the only route to
everywhere I want to go, which is why I
usually stay inside and rarely
dare to open my kitchen window.

From my kitchen window there's a very good view
of two-headed dog street, where old dustbin
bags grow into people, and where
handbags are liable to have nervous breakdowns.

Nervous breakdowns frequently occur on
two-headed dog street, and even I, who
do not live there, have been known to
participate from time to time.

From time to time I am forced to walk
down two-headed dog street, and the only way
to reach the other end is to
pretend that I am a two-headed dog.

The Gift

I am saving my money
to buy you a raw potato.

I will scrub it with my nailbrush
and bathe it in my basin.

I will cut out your initials
from its smooth, brown jacket.

I will gift-wrap it in pink paper
and tie it with pink ribbons.

I will place it in a shoe-box
on a bed of tissue paper.

I will deliver it to your doorstep,
wearing pink shoes.

You will stare at it crossly at first,
as if it were a baby.

You will take it inside quickly
to stop the neighbours staring.

You will not know where to put it.
You will be afraid to hold it.

You will hide it in your bedroom
to protect it from stray glances.

It will live in the furthest corner
forever, and embarrass you.

Mad Queen Hospital for Electrifying the Heart*

Welcome. My cocoa-buttered hands
Built these five rooms, undid this face,
Untangled all that once made sense.
The hall stands bare for compliments,
For chaos – an escape from peace.
So far so good. I'm in demand.

They bring their lives like powdered soup
For me to stir, and sniff, and drink;
The healing process, cruel to be
As cruel as they have been to me.
I am the one they have to thank.
I fill their rooms with scented soap.

Five at a time. The royal need
To charge their hearts, to be in charge,
Is almost physical, a craving.
I crave to save those not worth saving.
A mind once small that swells too large
Is happy as a hand grenade.

* The title of this poem is an extract from a poem called 'Telephone Directory'
by Harry Crosby.

After explosion, fully trained,
Their feet leave scars on bedroom rugs,
Their frenzy stains the corridors.
Clutching their hearts, expensive sores,
They pay the bill. I bleach the rags,
The ash, the lives they leave behind.

Doors beckon shut. My vacant palace,
Drooling, awaits the next arrivals.
Five relentless rooms to let
And nobody has caught me yet.
It's pure; a matter of survival,
No grudges held, no taint of malice.

Minding his Boots

He likes to walk around barefoot
while I mind his boots – the only part
of him which can stand still.

Pieces of broken glass and stones
don't seem to cut; his soles are tough,
dark like leather, skin socks.

Here is the trail of flat-crushed daisies
his going left behind, small white
and yellow crumbs in grass.

He is unreachable, framed
in an accidental afternoon
that lingers, hungry for souvenirs.

These boots which he leaves in my care
will belong to me longer than he will belong
to any earth, any air.

Something Coming

The pavement shone with news of something coming,
or just with rain. She took it as a warning,
identical to last time – first the humming,
then thunder, then his letter in the morning.

She did her best to see some sort of sense
in all these things, to make them fit together.
At the same time she laughed at the pretence
that love could be connected with the weather,

which can't be true, or life would be too frightening
to live. Next time she swore she'd go to bed
and not stay up to study trends of lightning
and wonder what, if anything, they said.

A Day Too Late

You meet a man. You're looking for a hero,
Which you pretend he is. A day too late
You realise his sex appeal is zero
And you begin to dread the second date.

You'd love to stand him up but he's too clever –
He knows by heart your work and home address.
Last night he said he'd stay with you forever.
You fear he might have meant it. What a mess!

That's when you start regretting his existence.
It's all his fault. You hate him with a passion.
You hate his love, his kindness, his persistence.
He's too intense. His clothes are out of fashion.

Shortly you reach the stage of desperation.
At first you thought about behaving well
And giving him an honest explanation.
Now all you want to say is 'Go to Hell',

And even that seems just a touch too gentle.
Deep down, the thing that makes you want to weep
Is knowing that you once felt sentimental
About this wholly unattractive creep.

Trainers All Turn Grey

(after Robert Frost's 'Nothing Gold Can Stay')

You buy your trainers new.
They cost a bob or two.
At first they're clean and white,
The laces thick and tight.
Then they must touch the ground –
(You have to walk around).
You learn to your dismay
Trainers all turn grey.

Another Filling

My sister knows my name and nothing else.
My mother knows my shoe size.
My father knows what kind of books I read.

My friends know where I drink.
My husband knows the colour of my hair.
My children know my rules.

My dentist knows I need another filling.
My boss knows I work late.
My cat knows that I'll share a turkey sandwich.

I know what makes me laugh.
I laugh at what they don't know.
They don't know very much about my dentist.

Introducing Vanity

A powder compact for a face,
White feet whose soles avoid the ground
But tread on lace,
Making a soft, material sound
In halls
Where heavy mirrors line the walls.

Bone china skin, pale jasmine breath;
In every sense an ornament.
Some pretty death
Will face her in the tournament.
A ghost,
She'll be more visible than most.

Her pointed features will impress
Insistent pouts upon the air.
She'll overdress
And wrap thick scarves around her hair;
Concealed
So that her shape might be revealed.

Stars will throw glitter on her jewels.
Inventor of the heart-shaped locket,
She collects fools
To put in her embroidered pocket.
She asks
For no-one to remove the masks.

Second Helping of Your Heart

1

I can't remember saying that I wanted this,
But these things happen. (Enter other platitudes.)
I was your midnight scrap. You left your haunted kiss
On my cold lips, without once changing attitudes.

A woman packs a suitcase in the south.
Calf-muscles ache. She may be feeling old tonight,
Or be in bed. Her understudy's mouth
Treats dirty fag-ends like small bars of gold tonight.

I can't remember mixing the ingredients.
Did I or did I not play any part in this?
(Enter a childhood training in obedience.)
Is there a second helping of your heart in this?

The inefficiency of most removal men
Is something that you cannot bear to think about.
Why I should bother chasing your approval when
I disapprove is something I must drink about.

Here, under chilly light and wooden beams,
My thumbnail is too long. It's like a talon.
Here is your parting gift: disruptive dreams
From four till seven. (Enter Woody Allen.)

2

If we examine ratios of power, praise
Becomes a farce. I start to doubt its origin
And its sincerity. Your leaning tower ways
Make bowls of women, fit for slopping porridge in.

Do I have any choice but to give way to you,
Here, in this echo-box? The shadows creep outside.
The sober cynic in me wants to say to you,
'Why bother with me, dear, when there are sheep outside?'

But you're too genuine, too off-the-cuff to be
Kept at a distance, treated with disparagement.
Let us not mention what you're old enough to be
Or that you're still not quite sure what your marriage meant.

So. Do you really think my work is saleable?
And will your confidence in me deflate a bit
If I declare my body unavailable,
All heavy, disbelieving five-foot-eight of it?

(Enter a fear of alcohol-dependency,
Tomorrow morning, what the hell I'll say to you.)
I can't risk heights and depths. I have a tendency
To step around such things. And so good day to you.

For the Following Reasons

Because strands of wool do not trail
from the sleeves of my jumper.

Because I would never stop reading a book
three pages before the end.

Because I brush teeth not tooth.

Because I wait for the aeroplane
to land before stepping outside.

Because I like to do things properly.

Because I like people to know what I mean
and do not stop talking or writing until they do.

Because I don't waste time on jigsaws
with only one piece,

or send letters without my signature,

or eat lunch without digesting it,

or brush all the hair to the left of my head,
ignoring what grows on the right.

Because I can only tolerate moments
if they are firmly lodged in hours.

Because I am orderly and extrapolate
neat patterns from the most uncertain things

you will be hearing from me again.

Two Rondels

THE END OF LOVE

The end of love should be a big event.
It should involve the hiring of a hall.
Why the hell not? It happens to us all.
Why should it pass without acknowledgement?

Suits should be dry-cleaned, invitations sent.
Whatever form it takes – a tiff, a brawl –
The end of love should be a big event.
It should involve the hiring of a hall.

Better than the unquestioning descent
Into the trap of silence, than the crawl
From visible to hidden, door to wall.

Get the announcements made, the money spent.
The end of love should be a big event.
It should involve the hiring of a hall.

MORE TROUBLE THAN FUN

We cannot undo what we've done
But we don't have to do any more.
What on earth are we doing it for
If it's so much more trouble than fun?

If you want, I can act like a nun.
I'll be meek and incredibly pure.
We cannot undo what we've done
But we don't have to do any more.

Just remember that you were the one
Who complained that your life was a bore.
Now you suddenly feel insecure.

Will it help if you panic and run?
We cannot undo what we've done
But we don't have to do any more.

Call Yourself a Poet

I called myself an architect,
Designed a huge sky-scraper.
How powerful it looked, erect
Upon my piece of paper.
Presto! The housing problem solved!
(I'd had no formal training.)
My pride and joy collapsed, dissolved,
The day it started raining.

I gave up architecture then
And called myself a vet.
My failure, time and time again,
To save a well-loved pet
Annoyed the RSPCA.
They went around campaigning
And I was forced to move away.
(I'd had no formal training.)

My next career was plumbing.
Easy enough, you'd think,
But I spent hours drumming
My fingers on the sink,
Scared to approach the toilet.
All blockages remained,
Which somehow seemed to spoil it.
(Perhaps I should have trained.)

I didn't dare to drive a van
So I became a poet.
I couldn't rhyme, make sense or scan
Yet no-one seemed to know it.
I knew that I had hit upon
My ultimate vocation
The day I met an Oxford don
Who praised my innovation.

Only last week I found myself
The subject of a lecture,
My book on some professor's shelf.
So who needs architecture,
Knowledge of water pipes? What fools
Dabble in surgery?
Oh, how restrictive! All those rules!
While verse, my friends, is free.

Amusing Myself

Here is the form I should have signed,
The book I should be reading.
Every attempt is undermined
By thoughts of you, stampeding.
I try to still them; am resigned
To not succeeding.

Here is the card I would have sent,
The fruit I would be peeling
If every second wasn't spent
On you, but while each feeling
Goes where its predecessor went
There'll be no healing.

Here are the words I'm scared to use.
You wouldn't catch me saying
This to your face, though I amuse
Myself and God by praying
That you'll be back; next time confuse
Me more by staying.

Differences

Not everyone who wears a hat
Is copying the Queen.
Not everything that's large and flat
Thinks it's a movie screen.
If every time I dress in blue
I imitate the sea,
It makes no difference what I do –
Nothing is down to me.

Not every dim, electric light
Would like to be the sun.
A water pistol doesn't quite
Mimic a loaded gun.
I do my best, I do my worst
With my specific heart –
God and the Devil got there first;
They had an early start.

Tomatoes can be round and red
Yet be distinct from Mars.
Not all the things above my head
Can be described as stars.
The world had better learn what's what
(If it remotely cares) –
A ladder is a ladder, not
A failed attempt at stairs.

The Answer

Why do you give the impression that you'd rather
not be loved? You almost tell people not to bother.
Why are you neither one thing nor the other?

Why do you fluctuate between ticks and crosses,
alternate between flippancy and neurosis?
Won't you confirm or contradict my guesses?

What is it that you do, by simply sitting
with your elbows raised, that makes me sick of waiting?
Why is your absence tantamount to cheating?

I know you're real, which means you must pay taxes,
catch colds and snore. I know you know what sex is.
Still, there is something in you that never mixes,

something that smells like the air in silver boxes.

It makes me suddenly afraid of asking,
suddenly sure of all the things I'm risking.

No Competition

I am in favour of a law being passed,
forbidding, to everyone but you, the use
of the word *whirlwind*.

I am in favour, also, of a law
being passed, restricting your vocabulary
to *whirlwind* only.

Here is how it would be in practical terms:
you, in the centre of a circular room,
unresentful, eyes closed, mouth open, and the word
whirlwind filling the room again and again.

Silence apart from this. No competition
from inferior words. Listeners on cushions
kissing the polished floor.

Friends Again

Let's sort this out. Make no more cherry
scones for the man that stole my jewels
and I'll stop spitting in your sherry.
Both of us have been fools.

Here, you can have my rope and pins
if you give up your hooks and nails
and we'll agree to wear wide grins
for subsequent betrayals.

Even a bond as firm as this
friendship cannot withstand attacks
if they are too direct; let's hiss
behind each other's backs.

In future, when I tread thick soil
into your house, I'll hide my feet,
and if you have to be disloyal
please try to be discreet.

The Mystery of the Missing

Think carefully. You sat down on a bench
and turned the pages of a small green book.
You were about to meet your friends for lunch.

> I turned the pages but I didn't look.
> It felt as if the bench was in mid-air.
> Whatever held me wouldn't put me back.

What happened next? You must have gone somewhere.
The wind was blowing hair across your face.
Perhaps you went inside and lit a fire.

> But people looked for me and found no trace
> inside or out. I saw the things they feared
> in the green book before I lost my place.

Surely they weren't afraid you'd disappeared?
Did they suspect you might have come to harm?
You could have reassured them with a word.

> I wanted to, but every word that came
> threatened to burn my mouth. I also knew
> that soon it would be over, I'd be home.

The sky closed in. You say you shrank, then grew,
then everything came back to you with ease.
You sat quite still, deciding what to do.

> Huge purple bruises covered both my knees
> But no-one acted like I'd been away.
> None of my friends asked what the matter was –

> Everyone else had had a normal day.

Miracles Start like This

Unlikely though it is
That you remember, let alone adore me,
Miracles start like this –
God, or yourself, or Jim
May fix it for me.

It's the impossibility
That makes recovered sight miraculous
And the same mystery
That unblinds eyes
Could do some work for us.

Perhaps a need like mine
For you would be considered too small-scale
To attract much divine
Concern, in which case
This appeal may fail.

I've heard of people walking into flames
And coming out unhurt. Though I hold tight to
Faith, I would like some names
As well, of lesser saviours
I could write to.

Nostalgia

At playgroup I was fond of chasing boys
And pulling hair, and breaking people's toys.
My teachers said that I was a deranged
And selfish child. What makes you think I've changed?

At school it was a matter of survival;
You flattened, or were flattened by, your rival.
Normal procedure was to swear and spit
At enemies. I made the most of it.

At sixth form college, fights were strictly banned.
Hate was forced underground. We schemed and planned
Behind each other's backs, and realised
That spite was more effective when disguised.

I've ended up at university
Where both aggression and hypocrisy
Are seen as qualities to be eschewed.
It's wrong to punch, spread rumours or be rude,

Or so I'm told. True, there is much less grief
When everyone behaves, but the relief
Of striking back has gone, as have the joys
Of pulling hair and breaking people's toys.

Two Love Poems

POEM FOR A VALENTINE CARD

You won't find any hints
Enclosed, no cryptic clues, no fingerprints,

Nothing about the gender,
Background or occupation of the sender.

Anonymous, unseen –
You're dealing with the all-time king or queen

Of undercover loves.
The author of this valentine wore gloves.

You could wear different shoes,
Lose all the worthwhile things you have to lose;

You could go mad and howl
From a high tree through darkness, like an owl –

No part of me would change
However sick you were, however strange.

Your future, near and distant,
Is safe, as long as I remain consistent.

If, one day, you commit
A crime, I'll burn all evidence of it.

When it arrives, my doom
Will be a red mist entering the room.

Early Bird Blues

I am the early bird.
I have worn out my shoes
Simply because I heard
First come was first to choose.
One of my talents is avoiding queues.

I never ask how long
I shall be made to wait.
I have done nothing wrong.
I don't exaggerate.
To state the obvious, I'm never late.

Why has the queue not grown?
Nobody hears me speak.
I stand here all alone
Which makes me look unique
But even so, the worm avoids my beak.

What do the others know?
Have I been told a lie?
Why don't I turn and go?
I still know how to fly,
But, damn, I want that worm. I don't know why.

Your Street Again

'Guess who I saw last night?' was all she said.
That, and the answer (you), was all it took,
And now I'm leafing through my A–Z
To find your street again. I had to look

Four years ago, and memorise the way:
Palatine, Central, Burton – halfway there.
I don't intend to visit you today
As I did then, and so I shouldn't care

Which road comes after which and where they lead.
I do, though. I repeat them name by name.
My house is here and yours is there. I need
To prove the space between them stays the same.

Three Short Poems

A SOUL

And if I have a soul my soul is green
And if it sings it doesn't sing to me
And if it loves it loves externally
Both what it has and what it hasn't seen

And if it's green it may as well be high
And if ambition doesn't give it height
And if it only rises with a fight
Against itself and not against the sky

If all the force it uses leaves me free
This proves it not just definite but right

CATEGORIES

Some things resist division into parts:
The ventricles and atria of hearts –
The one is at a loss without the other.
The dead son slowly kills the living mother.

The dumbest mouths are those that miss their tongues.
The coldest air is far away from lungs.
Freedom is not what separation brings.
One person takes the bird and one the wings.

Each of us joins a different category
And what is in between ought not to be.

THE THREE COME-UPPANCES

She knew a man who didn't quite recover
She owns a villa in the France of Spain
Your terraced husband has a penthouse lover
There's a come-uppance cruising down the lane

She hopes your terrace doesn't quite recover
She's confident her clothes cost more than yours
She introduced your husband to his lover
There's a come-uppance banging at the doors

She's feeling fragile just before the scene
There's a come-uppance in the fax machine

The Trouble with Keeping in Touch

In case you've ever asked yourself how long
A girl can sit and chew a ball-point pen,
Put down some words and then decide they're wrong
And cross the whole lot out and start again;

In case you've wondered how the record stands,
Take it from me (I know because I hold it) –
It's infinite; it constantly expands.
The truth can change just when you think you've told it.

Whatever may have happened to us both
Since I last smiled and waved and said goodnight to you,
Our lives continue growing, and the growth
Makes it impossible for me to write to you.

Ghazal

Imagine that a man who never writes
Walks on the planet Mars in cricket whites

Looking for signs of life which isn't there.
He walks through hot red days and dark red nights

Across a surface which is rough and bare.
He feels confused; he's come to see the sights

But there are none, and nobody to share
His empty mouth, his sudden fear of heights.

Nine of his cigarettes are going spare.
The tenth is for himself, and that he lights.

Something's familiar now. He starts to swear.
He stumbles through bizarre, one-sided fights.

Meanwhile you're stuck on Earth without the fare.
In any case, there are no scheduled flights.

And all the love you send is lost in air,
And all your words stick in the sky like kites.

Superstitions

I refuse to share my superstitions with anyone.
You can keep shoes off the table, walk around ladders,
Throw spilt salt over your shoulder, salute single magpies –
My behaviour, although insane, is at least original.

I look out of windows but never look into them.
I guard against colds with a fake Scandinavian accent
And I know I will have good luck when my path is crossed
Not by a black cat, but by a Chinese man called Norman.

This has happened twice in my life (same Norman both times).
Long fingernails are a bad omen. When I last grew mine
I found some unexplained underwear in my laundry bag
And was followed home by a man with a bushy moustache.

I'm telling the truth. I would never lie on a Friday.
This is not a superstition but what I was taught
By my mother, who used to say if you lose your cat
Give a hedgehog a saucer of milk and hope for the best.

The Usherette

When no-one tore my ticket up or said
No smoking – any seats except the red
I realised the usherette was dead.

A tray of ice-creams dangled at her side.
Her eyes were open and her hair was tied
Up at the back, just like before she died.

I gathered, from the coldness of her skin,
Death had occurred during the Gordon's Gin
Advertisement. Latecomers, trailing in,

Deposited their tickets in her palm
As, one by one, they passed her stiff, white arm
Showing no sign of interest or alarm.

They took their seats. I crouched down in the aisle,
Next to the usherette. Her frozen smile
Wouldn't release my stare. After a while

I fell asleep. What happened next was weird –
When I woke up her corpse had disappeared.
Nobody would believe me now, I feared.

After the film I waited by the door
Trying to memorise each face I saw
And then I left, since I could do no more.

Love Me Slender

LOVELY LESLEY LOST SIX STONE AND WON HER MAN
(headline from The Sun, *30 June 1993)*

You have to be size ten to get a bloke.
You must be slim, petite, and never podgy.
Since Stout is out you're left with Diet Coke
And other things that taste extremely dodgy.

You must be thin. Don't make me say it twice.
Size ten, or even twelve, but never fatter.
You may, in other ways, be very nice
But if you're overweight it doesn't matter.

You have to shed the pounds. It's such a drag.
You can't rely on brains or sense of humour.
It isn't true that many men will shag
Virtually anyone – that's just a rumour.

You need a model's figure, skin and bone,
Straight up and down without a single curve,
Unless you want to end up on your own,
Which, frankly, would be just what you deserve.

Morning Has Broken

The shark in *Jaws* was a lovable household pet.
Butch Cassidy and Sundance didn't die.
Scarlett and Rhett
did not split up. They gave it another try.

And you're a good egg, safe bet,
real brick. You're an honest guy.

The encounter was not so brief.
The bodies were never snatched.
Clyde Barrow wasn't a thief.

You're available, unattached –
no partner to give you grief.
We are well-matched.

Bergman and Bogart got back together
after the end of *Casablanca*.

I'm not at the end of my tether
and you're not a wanker.

As for last night,
neither my feelings nor my drinks were mixed
and it looks the same in the light.
Morning is fixed.

Skipping Rhyme for Graduates

I've got the motive.
I've got the stamina.
I'm going to kill
The external examiner.

Let crows and vultures
Pick at the carcass
After I've murdered
The stingiest of markers.

Bring out the bin-bags.
Bring out the spades.
Bring down the evil sod
Who brings down the grades.

Give me an alibi.
Give me a gun.
Wanted a first
But I got a two-one.

Just missed a first
By a fragment of a fraction.
Justice is called for,
Justice and action.

What a bloody miser!
What a bloody crook!
Won't mark another paper.
Won't write another book.

Won't see his bloody name
In another bloody journal.
Bye-bye, examiner.
Bye-bye, external.

Mountains out of Small Hills

Dogs are objecting to the word dogmatic,
the use of certain phrases – barking mad,
dog in the manger. Equally emphatic
are other species. Rats and snakes have had

enough of being symbols of deceit
and treachery. They say there's no excuse,
and there are fish protesting on the street
at being linked with alcohol abuse.

You couldn't taunt a coward nowadays
with 'scaredy-cat' or 'chicken'. Cock-and-bull
stories have been renamed. Nobody says
'God, she's a cow!' Nobody pulls the wool

over another person's eyes – the lambs
have seen to that. Nobody rabbits on.
Nor has there been a ramraid since the rams
petitioned parliament. We do not swan

around, get goosebumps; nothing gets our goat.
No cricket player ever scores a duck.
Once we were free with what we said and wrote.
Now we make do with swear-words. Bollocks. Fuck.

Reconstruction

Most of the witnesses were pissed.
The room is as it was before.
They do their best, but they persist
In seeing only what they saw
And missing what they've always missed.

They close their eyes. They walk around
But nothing seems to spring to mind.
How will they know when they have found
Whatever they're supposed to find?
Is it a smell? Is it a sound?

They do not know and cannot guess
What might be meant by evidence.
Since none of them would dare confess
Their presence here makes little sense,
But they are happy, more or less,

With things exactly as they are.
The first impression is the last.
If there is truth it lies too far
Away for them to reach. The past
Is like a disappearing star.

The Hero and the Girl Next Door

This story has at least one side.
The source is quite reliable.
The hero did his best. He tried,
But it was not a viable
Prospect, and so he burned his boats,
He cut his losses, changed his mind,
Dry-cleaned his most attractive coats
And left the girl next door behind.

His Christmas list had shed a name.
The girl next door had shed some tears,
But she was utterly to blame,
Had been, in fact, for several years.
Rewind. The lady vanishes.
Press stop, fast forward, then eject.
And what a silly girl she is.
And does she honestly expect…

So this is provocation, then,
And this is what they call just cause
And this is how you see it when
The hero is a friend of yours.
Another soldier saves his skin.
Another wrinkle ironed out.
You bet. You roll the dice. You win.
There is no reasonable doubt.

An Aerial View

Flight 608. The woman to my right
Has hardly touched the meal Air France provided.
She prods it with her fork as though she might,
Probably won't, but hasn't quite decided.

She eyes my empty tray with vague distaste –
I ate it all, and we were given loads.
She's proud of her restraint, her slender waist.
Neither will help her if the plane explodes.

She's frowning at my bottle of champagne,
Perhaps because it's only 8 a.m.,
But I don't care. When I am on a plane
My motto is 'enjoy myself – stuff them'.

Long-face can stick to water all the way,
That's up to her. I don't intend to slum it.
I'm pissed. She never drinks before midday.
Irrelevant distinction, if we plummet.

Last chance, perhaps, for grub and heavy drinking.
One shouldn't miss it. Here's what I advise:
Light up a fag, and concentrate on thinking
An aeroplane is just a pub that flies.

Absence Makes the Heart Grow Henry

Ann was the love of Colin's life
Until the day he went to meet her.
Later she became his wife
But absence makes the heart grow Peter.

Jack was obsessed with Debbie's writing.
Then one day he caught the train
And found the woman less exciting.
Absence makes the heart grow Jane.

I love you when you're not around.
If we come face to face again we
Stand to lose by being found,
For absence makes the heart grow Henry.

The Only Point is Decimal

Ninety per cent of places are not worth going.
Ninety per cent of jobs are not worth doing.
Ninety per cent of men are not worth knowing.
Ninety per cent of women are not worth screwing.

An attitude like yours must take some practice.
Part apathetic, mostly condescending,
Lukewarm then spiky, vichyssoise-cum-cactus,
That's you, my friend. Or are you just pretending?

Ninety per cent of books are not worth reading.
Ninety per cent of songs are not worth singing.
Ninety per cent of advice is not worth heeding.
Ninety per cent of numbers are not worth ringing.

Life passes by, but you are not impressed.
You'd rather be a lonely couch potato
Than compromise. There's no point getting dressed
For anyone less erudite than Plato.

Ninety per cent of chances are not worth taking.
Ninety per cent of corners are not worth turning.
Ninety per cent of hands are not worth shaking.
Ninety per cent of candles are not worth burning.

And all that I can think is what a shame.
What are the odds you'll wonder where I went?
The chances of you knowing why I came?
Point zero zero zero one per cent.

A Really Tacky Tourist Beach

Policemen wink and I relax.
I drive and drive but never see
A gift shop that's museum-free.
A sign beside the road says 'Snacks'.

The perfect morning for a race,
But there is no-one in my wake
And nobody to overtake.
I need another car to chase.

I drink and swim just like a fish.
One of these days I hope to reach
A really tacky tourist beach.
The traffic lights may grant my wish.

I have a stone called Sheriff John
And when I sing he sings along.
We do our favourite Beach Boys song.
Our skin is rough, our voices gone.

I pick a star and watch it rise;
Look left, look right. The mirror shows
A grinning mouth, a powdered nose
But nobody I recognise.

The Fairy Never Came to Get My Teeth

How can I help? I don't know when to clap
And when to throw a fit. It's not my day.
I've got a notebook sitting on my lap.
I can't get up until it goes away.

How do the neighbours know your bones are brittle?
I hear it from above you and beneath.
How's this for relevance: when I was little
The fairy never came to get my teeth.

I'm one of them, no longer one of us.
I haven't got the knack of self-expression
Like others have. I never make a fuss
Or jump the queue. I'm in the wrong profession.

The sawn-off shotgun in your biscuit tin,
The headless rodent in your Christmas stocking,
May drive me mad, but I will not barge in.
We're quaint round here. We still believe in knocking.

The smartest pupil in the haystack class
Pontificates all night: attack, defend…
Meanwhile there's no-one sweeping up the glass.
What you need most is not another friend,

Another eager face behind the door
To make you circulate a false address.
I keep away. Ask yourself who cares more.
A bigger crowd creates a bigger mess.

What do I think about an early grave?
Head-on collision with a wall or tree?
I think it's neither glamorous nor brave.
You need a louder audience than me.

You need a quiet night without a row.
You need a holiday. You need a fling.
(I hear my mother say *Be careful now*
And my reply: *I am becarefulling*.)

Leaving the house, dizzy from lack of lunch,
I pass two cold burritos in a trilby.
Each flippant story packs a careful punch.
It's not your day. I doubt it ever will be.

Fish Tony's Chips

Fish Tony's Chips. The marble god has eyes.
His handshake is a cupboard on the wall
In which a cabbage rots and changes size.

I constantly outgrow my overall.
Try something new. I hope you don't succeed.
Reserve that room for me or not at all.

We do not yet have all the words we need.
Check your thesaurus. Where's the word that means
To go out looking like a centipede?

To wear clean knickers under dirty jeans
And hold a bottle neck between your lips?
But what is happening behind the scenes?

The marble god has eyes. Fish Tony's Chips.

Bafield Load

Her desperation never showed.
For years she lived on Bafield Load

according to the envelope
that brought the final loss of hope.

From time to time she'd blink and shout:
'There's nothing to be dead about!'

but they'd already sprayed her grave
with cheap ex-boyfriend aftershave.

The Keyboard and the Mouse

I am myself and in my house
But if I had my way
I'd be the keyboard and the mouse
Under your hands all day.

I'd be the C prompt on the screen.
We could have had some fun
This morning, if I'd only been
Word Perfect 5.1.

I'd be your hard and floppy discs,
I'd be your laser jet,
Your ampersands and asterisks –
I'd be in Somerset

Rotating on your swivel chair.
The journey takes a while
But press return and I'll be there.
Do not delete this file.

The Safest Place

It's a hygienic lovers' tiff
That starts with if and only if
And tails off like a doctor's note.
How could you write the things you wrote,

Scaremongering? I'm sure we'll live.
Thank God my job's repetitive.
It keeps me calm – no hurt, no games.
I type a list of authors' names,

Relish the thought of getting bored.
I'm busy here. I can't afford
To fall apart or fall behind.
Everywhere else you're on my mind;

Work has become the safest place.
This catalogue, this database,
Proves, in a way, that life goes on.
Beaumont, Francis. Fletcher, John.

Triskaidekaphobia

Is it as easy as you make it sound?
You tell me not to cry on your account.
You didn't cry. I doubt you even frowned.
You sleep too easily when I'm around.
If I'm too much, are you the right amount?

This is about as open as I get.
Gram Parsons said love hurts and I agree
Although I haven't said I love you yet
And therefore have no right to be upset
Because you don't say anything to me.

We've really taken safety to extremes.
Reluctance makes us both insensitive.
They may come true, but would we call them dreams?
We're playground captains, calmly picking teams,
And even if there's nothing to forgive

You're hardly what a nice young girl expects,
If I can still describe myself as such –
Prostitutes, dogs and strange religious sects,
Your special drug and alcohol effects.
The message on your back reads please don't touch.

I see a threat in every paragraph,
Subject each letter to analysis.
I try and fail (you just can't get the staff)
To resurrect the flirt that made you laugh
But find her taking all your jokes amiss,

And all your views on dolls and boxing rings.
It's good to see your well-proportioned mind
Is on top form and full of different things.
Were you a child who didn't fall off swings
Unless there was a mattress close behind?

All right, I'm being totally unfair
But silence always makes me want to rant,
Like sneaking through the nothing to declare
Gate at the airport. I can hardly bear
Your morning walks. You're far too much like Kant.

A bit more truth over a few more days
And maybe panic would give way to sense.
Look at me now. I take a simple phrase
And blow it up in twelve pedantic ways,
Not out of spite, merely as self-defence.

This dot to dot is less than we deserve,
One of the many things I wish I'd said.
Until such time as I can find the nerve
I'll walk in ways that make the traffic swerve
And try to stop you getting out of bed.

When Will You Come and Identify My Body?

When will you come and identify my body?
It had better be soon or I might just take it amiss.
When will you come and identify my body?
Men basically do what they want, and I've only just realised this.

It was silly of me to drown in a shallow river,
Too small a gesture to impress the boys.
It was silly of me to drown in a shallow river.
They are either silent, or else they are making their football noise.

I would like to be buried with my shampoo and conditioner.
Once I was self-obsessed and even clean.
I would like to be buried with my shampoo and conditioner.
I'm aware that the cricket highlights start at eleven fifteen.

I have been deacidified and boxed.
You shouldn't have left me. You shouldn't have gone to the bar.
I have been deacidified and boxed.
You'll find me in pepper and pickle. You'll find me under the car

Or creeping up behind you with a trowel.
Are you a garlic crusher or a torch?
I'm creeping up behind you with a trowel.
You would never change. You would never redecorate the porch.

It's clear to me from the way you keep escaping
(Into halls, through doors) that you will never be ready.
It's clear, from me to the way you keep escaping.
When, though? When will you come? Will you come and identify
my body?

Hotels Like Houses

Three Hundred Years for Me

He spent last summer in a caravan
With four professors and a Polish priest.
He spent this morning with the Seafood Man
And lunchtime at a window cleaners' feast.

He spent the weekend in a bungalow
Owned by a bloke who used to teach me French.
This evening he'll be at the early show
Of some new film, then on a cold park bench

With ski instructors from the Cairngorm slopes.
He'll spend tomorrow in a parking lot
With a Duke's niece who writes the horoscopes
For women's magazines. Then, when he's got

An hour, maybe half an hour free
I'll make him wait three hundred years for me.

Where is Talcott Parsons Now?

(Talcott Parsons, American sociologist, 1902–1979)

Could a man in your position
Ever love a girl like me?
Would you have to get permission
From the aristocracy?
Just a normal girl, no dowry,
With a house which, at first glance,
Looks like something drawn by Lowry?
Would we ever stand a chance?

Am I utterly deluded
Or could such a love exist?
Would I have to be included
In the Civil Honours List,
Hang about with landed gentry,
Or would access be denied?
Would there be a firm no entry
To all persons from Moss Side?

Are your exes all princesses
Who could spot a pea with ease?
Do they wear designer dresses
And have dinner with MPs?
Are they many times my betters
With their titles, wealth and fame?
Does each one of them have letters
Queueing up beside her name?

Would it be too much to handle?
Would your folks rewrite their wills?
Would it lead, perhaps, to scandal
Or some parliamentary bills?
Would the penalties be hefty?
Will we know until we've tried?
Is the heart a closet lefty
That will not be stratified?

I remember how I hated
Sociology at school
And I've only ever dated
Normal people as a rule.
Masses loving other masses
Maybe never need to learn
That ye olde social class is
Still a relevant concern.

Can mobility be hurried?
Where is Talcott Parsons now
When I need him, when I'm worried?
Do the text books not allow
For a man in your position
Just to have the briefest whirl
(In the Mills & Boon tradition)
With an ordinary girl?

Do I Look Sick?

The gap you leave beside me is unfillable.
I have had just enough of you to care.
I wish your name contained an extra syllable.
Please do not ever shave or cut your hair.

If only there was altogether more of you,
Though some would argue there's already quite a lot.
I'm hoping to deprive the foreign poor of you.
I've no desire to stay at home and write a lot

Nor will I be donating you to charity.
Let's face it – I've become proprietorial.
I don't need someone mystical or taroty
To tell me this weekend is a memorial

To last weekend and to the time I spent with you.
You left too soon and I was in a hurry so
I failed to mention maybe sharing rent with you.
Do I look sick? I eat a lot of curry though.

Each morning is a painful anniversary.
I stank of smoke and scotch but you smelled clean to me.
If I could get a special grant or bursary
I'd fill in forms, explaining what you mean to me.

I asked for nothing at the time. How cool I was,
How casual. I'm sorry for misleading you.
All subsequent events show what a fool I was.
I should have known that I would end up needing you.

I act like I'm some expert on relationships.
Right now I'm waiting for my life to mend a bit,
Eating a bag of Piccadilly Station chips
And writing this. You'll never hear the end of it.

In the Bone Densitometry Room

I could say that my life is my own
When you ask where I've been and with whom
But my voice has the tone
Of a powdery bone
In the bone densitometry room.

I could say there are rats in my throne.
I'm a helium bride with no groom,
Just a motorway cone,
And I crush like a bone
In the bone densitometry room.

It is not what you seek to postpone.
It is not what you wrongly assume.
This erogenous zone
Is as smooth as a bone
In the bone densitometry room.

Are my feelings as commonly known
As a raid on a high-rise in Hulme?
Are they tapping my phone?
Am I really a bone
In the bone densitometry room?

If my cover's already been blown
They can sweep me away with a broom.
When you leave me alone
I'm a shivering bone
In the bone densitometry room.

Neither Home nor Dry

No need to put your magazine away
If there's an article you want to read;
I could just sit and look at you all day.
Were you about to speak to me? No need.
My minimum is very bare indeed.

I'm happy eating breakfast on my own
Knowing that you are in a room nearby,
Smugly asleep. I'm happy to postpone
Thought and decision, question and reply
For now, since I am neither home nor dry.

You want to stir your drink? I'll fetch a spoon.
I'll wear my heels down looking at the sights
Because you say I should. We're leaving soon.
I watch the pattern form. I may have rights
But no time has been set aside for fights.

Soon I'll be in my favourite service station
(Well-named, because it is a welcome break),
Eating a slice of sickly *Fudge Temptation*
As usual. With such a lot at stake
It's comforting to recognise a cake.

Hotels like Houses

She is the one who takes a shine
to ceilings and to floors,
whose eye finds room for every line
scratched on the wardrobe doors.

She thinks in terms of thick red rope
around the bed, a plaque
above the hardened bathroom soap.
He's always first to pack.

If their affair has awkward spells,
what's bound to cause the rows is
that he treats houses like hotels
and she, hotels like houses.

From A to B (when B is Miles from A)

He sold his car the day before they met
Not knowing she would live so far away.
Perhaps he would have sold it anyway
If he was broke, or if his mind was set

On doing so, but it is hard to get
From A to B when B is miles from A.
He sold his car the day before they met
Not knowing she would live so far away –

A fact she won't forgive and can't forget.
Ideally, she'd see him every day.
Whether he feels the same, it's hard to say.

People with cars can have affairs, no sweat.
He sold his car the day before they met,
Not knowing she would live so far away.

Do Detached Houses Want to be Detached?

Do detached houses want to be detached
Or would they rather get beyond their gates
And team up with a dozen box-like mates,
Be smaller, cheaper homes on rough estates
Where it's not safe to walk, where bags are snatched?

Are they quite happy self-contained and proud
Or would they like to slide along the road
(New meaning to the term *no fixed abode*)
To somewhere with a less exclusive code?
Would they exchange their privacy for loud

Car alarms ringing almost every night?
For now they stand where no one steals a car.
Would they be safer staying where they are,
Wiser, as well? Too wise to move too far?
You think they would. You think you know you're right.

Altering the Angle

Quick, summon up your out-of-bed persona;
Start acting like you met me at a conference
Ages ago. Throw in a bit of indifference.
This month's adventure stars the cowboy loner,
And, look, it's almost time to do something spontaneous.

For all your talk of changes and the future
You wouldn't dream of altering the angle
Of your ponytail, relinquishing the single
Newspaper life. Under that cloak of culture
Your past consumes your present like a vulture.

I'm flexible, but why should I adapt
To being systematically ignored
By somebody whose scores don't make the board?
And as for warmth you might as well be wrapped
In clingfilm on an isolation ward.

Proud of how unemotional you are,
You coast along – never a peak or trough –
And I'm your novelty inside a jar;
You count the seconds of my wearing off,
Talk about how you'd like to travel far
Away from me. I hope the sea is rough.

So, what's the next meticulously planned
Escapade going to be? Will you expand
Your consciousness, experiment with lust,
Make a few notes and think you've got it sussed,
The science of excitement in your hand?

Well, here's goodbye. Experiment with that.
You're far too big a space for me to fill,
And even with the greatest strength of will
I can't hallucinate a rolling hill
On land that is predominantly flat.

When He's at Home

A patch provokes the lazy eye,
Pillars support the dome.
I say his name and friends reply
Who's he when he's at home?

He's a performing art on stage.
At work he's smart and busy.
He's Times New Roman on the page.
When he's at home, who is he?

He's the road atlas man in cars.
On fairground rides he's dizzy.
He's wet in rain and drunk in bars.
When he's at home, who is he,

When there is nothing that provokes
And when there's no support?
Nothing. The show is over, folks,
And sooner than I thought.

Slow Start, Weak End

Dirty. That's what you think and how you smell.
Slow start, weak end, and now the late, deluded
Head of the fan club rings a tarnished bell.
Don't wonder what went wrong. That's easy – you did.
You're smiling at me now. What's the occasion?
I watch you as you go into remission.
My touch is more and more of an abrasion
And we will never find the right position.
Nothing rubs off on me; I take a shower
Mainly because there's nowhere else to hide.
If you have good points, princes in the tower
Is all they are. You keep them shut inside.
I need a break. You know the kind I mean:
Like the weekend. Like disinfectant. Clean.

Two Sonnets

DARLING SWEATHEART

He couldn't spell. The letters were addressed
to *Darling Sweatheart,* though he acted mean
when I was with him. Probably the best
present he gave me was some margarine –

a tub of Stork, half full. It wasn't wrapped.
He shrugged and said *You might as well have this.*
He'd find excuses, say his lips were chapped
in an attempt to dodge my weekly kiss.

He'd made a comprehensive wedding plan
involving just the two of us. No way
were guests allowed. His dog would be Best Man.
I dithered. *What a life* he used to say,

Let's have a kid. If we get skint, we'll sell it.
He wasn't bad. It's just the way I tell it.

CREDIT FOR THE CARD

She took the credit for the card I sent.
It's bad enough that you are hers, not mine.
How dare she, after all the time I spent
Choosing and writing out your Valentine,
Pretend it came from her, after the date
And its significance had slipped her mind?
She saw her chance before it was too late
And claimed my card – mysterious, unsigned –
Became the face behind my question mark.
Now there's too much at stake. She can't confess.
She has conspired to keep you in the dark
Which fact, she knows, would make you like her less.
Her lips are sealed. She lied and she forgot
Valentine's Day. I didn't. Mine are not.

Fair to Say

It's fair to say you own a boat. It's yours.
Nothing luxurious. A rowing boat.
First it springs holes and then you lose the oars.
It's when the thing can barely stay afloat
Let alone speed you off to foreign shores –
At that point you no longer have a boat.

You rent a flat, a corrugated box,
No fancy furnishings, no welcome mat.
One day the landlord changes all the locks.
A dog moves in. It tries to kill your cat.
It's when the door stays closed, despite your knocks –
At that point you no longer have a flat.

You've got a boss. You've worked for him for years.
He is a firm, authoritative boss
Until one day the office disappears.
You ask him what to do. He's at a loss.
He looks away and covers up his ears –
At that point you no longer have a boss.

As for your man, the things he used to do
Like smile and speak, watch movies, make a plan,
Listen to music, kiss – to name a few –
He's given up, as if some kind of ban
Were on them all. When somebody who blew
Hot now blows cold and you've done all you can –
At that point you no longer have a man.

When his turned back makes one bed feel like two –
At that point you no longer have a clue.

The During Months

Like summer in some countries and like rain
in mine, for nuns like God, for drunks like beer,
like food for chefs, for invalids like pain,
you've occupied a large part of the year.

The during months to those before and since
would make a ratio of ten to two,
counting the ones spent trying to convince
myself there was a beating heart in you

when diagrams were all you'd let me see.
Hearts should be made of either blood or stone,
or both, like mine. There's still December free –
the month in which I'll save this year, alone.

Three Poems about Cars and Driving

IN THE BLIND SPOT

I check the rearview mirror. Has she seen us?
And is that *her* face in the car behind?
And does she stare from Polos and Cortinas,
Or is it guilt that's playing with my mind?
And if so, why? It's not as though I've chucked her.
This lesson hardly constitutes a breach
Of trust. I'm only with this new instructor
While she is unavailable to teach.
But still, I should have said, I should have told her.
Is that her car, about to overtake,
Or in the blind spot, just behind my shoulder?
In all three mirrors as I hit the brake?
And while I fight these visions, how the hell
Am I supposed to learn to drive as well?

SLOW IT RIGHT DOWN

Nobody gets priority with you
So all concerned must do the best they can:
Be safe and stop, be brave and charge on through –
You are an unmarked crossroads of a man.

Some men I know are double yellow lines
Or traffic lights for everyone to see.
I'm practised when it comes to give way signs
But unmarked crossroads are a mystery

And this time I shall do it by the book,
Slow it right down and read my highway code;
Before reversing, take one final look –
An unmarked crossroads down an unknown road.

FOR B440 UBU

On the horizon there's a car.
I do not often look that far
But for my postman's car I do,
For B440 UBU.

Until the postman comes, I wait.
It regularly makes me late,
This waiting for a distant view
Of B440 UBU.

My boyfriend tries to make me leave
The house, refuses to believe
I've seen the shape, the size, the hue
Of B440 UBU.

He says the car's too far away.
He adds that if I'm wrong, I may
Be waiting here an hour or two
For B440 UBU.

I tell him I can see that far.
I recognise my postman's car.
I know that what I say is true –
That's B440 UBU.

The Learner

Your only hope of knowing how he feels
is wading through the electronic mail.
He'll walk away with feet like cutting wheels,
turning the ground on which you stand to shale
      when his heart peels
off, like a stick-on L-plate in a heavy gale.

This man believes in dragons breathing fire.
When he stands still, you'll hear his shaking bones
and when he moves he's like a rolling tyre
over a box of semi-precious stones,
      faster and higher
than L-plates loose in twenty-mile-an-hour zones.

Be careful of the drinks he wants to buy
if he does not at first appear thick skinned.
Soon as you tell yourself he's scared or shy
he'll be the board where all your hopes are pinned.
      Then watch him fly
off, like a truant L-plate carried by the wind.

The Treasurer

He's much too busy to appreciate
my effort in his clean and perfect pages.
I watch him work himself into a state
over this year's accounts, the rise in wages,
and see it in his face each time we speak –
not worth an extra twenty-seven pounds a week.

I tell him that he's under too much stress
and ought to let me do another day.
He shakes his head because it costs him less,
wanting my time but not enough to pay
for more of it, and who am I to gripe?
Plenty of people can stuff envelopes and type.

How can I tell him that I'd work for free
just for the chance to touch his winter coat?
Some treasurer. He doesn't treasure me.
I wonder how the business stays afloat,
for he must lack investment sense, my boss,
running his greatest asset at so great a loss.

Lusting after Walter Knife

They mention him without intent
And you pretend you haven't heard
Anything more than what was meant
Because his name's a household word.

Imagine – loving Peter Chair
Would make deciding where to sit
Almost impossible to bear
If you connected him with it,

Or lusting after Walter Knife –
One move to spread your margarine
Might make you want to stab his wife;
Not what things are but what they mean

To you, so dig a hole and hide
Unless his name is Pete or Loam
And if the man's called Mountainside
You might be better off at home.

To Whom it May Concern at the Whalley Range Driving Test Centre

Please don't regard this as a threat.
We'll be the best of friends, I bet,
Though up to now we've never met
And I'd just like the chance to get
Some feelings off my chest,

Which won't take very long to read.
The point is this: I must succeed.
I'll never drink and drive or speed.
I really want and really need
To pass my driving test,

And, well, if God forbid I fail
I'll stand outside your house and wail,
Circle your place of work and trail
Black L-plates from a black gauze veil.
I'll be the petrol guest

At every gathering you host,
Proposing a malignant toast,
A sickly, seatbelt-wearing ghost,
Liking you least instead of most.
I'll never let you rest

And may your Fiat Tipo burn.
Sorry. That sounds a little stern.
My nerves are bad. Tonight I learn
Left hand reverse and three point turn
So wish me all the best.

The Pros and the Cons

He'll be pleased if I phone to ask him how he is.
It will make me look considerate and he likes considerate people.

He'll be reassured to see that I haven't lost interest,
which might make him happy and then I'll have done him a favour.

If I phone him right now I'll get to speak to him sooner
than I will if I sit around waiting for him to phone me.

He might not want to phone me from work in case someone hears
him
and begins (or continues) to suspect that there's something between us.

If I want to and don't, aren't I being a bit immature?
We're both adults. Does it matter, with adults, who makes the first
move?

But there's always the chance he'll back off if I come on too strong.
The less keen I appear, the more keen he's likely to be,

and I phoned him twice on Thursday and once on Friday.
He must therefore be fully aware that it's his turn, not mine.

If I make it too easy for him he'll assume I'm too easy,
while if I make no effort, that leaves him with more of a challenge.

I should demonstrate that I have a sense of proportion.
His work must come first for a while and I shouldn't mind waiting.

For all I know he could have gone off me already
and if I don't phone I can always say, later, that I went off him first.

Into His Plans

The truth, which on my more possessive days
Lurks in the background, spoiling all the fun,
That I am not the only game he plays,
Neither am I the most important one,
I've always known. I knew before I fell
Into his plans. I knew because he said,
And, flattered that he wanted me as well,
I didn't wish he wanted me instead
At that stage. Now I'm feeling discontent
And longing for a more familiar mess –
Having been many people's main event,
People who've hurt me more and liked me less
Than he does – also knowing that it's wrong
To think this way, not thinking it for long.

On the Silver Side

However you may be under a different bridge,
under this one you're luminous and round,
watch-faced or moon-faced, split, on the silver side,
glowing right through me as I begin sprouting wires.

I have looked for you under the bridge of the curling stones,
under the oily bridge and under the fence
that believes it's a bridge. You aren't under any of those,
however you may be under a different bridge,

one made of shells and crowns and packs of cards,
coliseums and changing rooms, but you'd better not be
under my bridge wishing you were somewhere else.
However you may be under a different bridge.

Preventative Elegy

There will not be a burial,
There will not be a wake.
No ashes will be sprinkled
Over the stream or lake.
There won't be a cremation,
A coffin or a shroud.
No hearse will park along the road –
Your death is not allowed.

There will not be a graveyard,
There'll be no marble stone
Bearing a carved endearment.
No flesh will shrink to bone
And in the town that loves you
There'll be no sobbing crowd.
No one inherits anything –
Your death is not allowed.

No grief will need to be disguised
As just a bit upset.
No one will wonder whether to
Remember or forget
Or which would cause the greater pain,
And whether we laughed or rowed
Last time will be irrelevant –
Your death is not allowed.

Others will die instead of you.
A fixed amount must die
(If there are quotas with these things)
And strangers' wives will cry
But I will have no need to say
I loved you and was proud
To be what I have been to you –
Your death is not allowed.

Person Specification

The ideal candidate for the position
of soulmate to the all-important you
should say she loves you, of her own volition,
every five minutes, and it should be true.

She must be motivated and ambitious
but feminine. She will be good at art,
at homely things. Her meals should be nutritious.
The ideal candidate will win your heart

with her prowess in bed. She will look stunning
in public, turn at least ten heads per day.
She should do most of (if not all) the running
and be prepared for marriage straight away.

Points will be lost for boring occupations,
excessive mood swings, drugs and other men.
To those who fail, your deep commiserations.
This post will not be advertised again.

The Sight of Mares

Either a dark horse, not a horse at all,
or else a horse resentful of the label,
at giddy-ups he turns to face the wall.
He says he's never been inside a stable.

I take his word for it (he ought to know),
but others disagree and say he moves
just like a horse. Explain, then, why he's so
uncomfortable with the idea of hooves

and why he shudders at the sight of mares
and all the other things you can't explain.
Four legs he may have – so do beds and chairs,
but something makes you call his hair a mane

and you imagine he must have a tail
though you would never say so to his face,
not when he puts his saddle up for sale
and says he hasn't heard about the race

in which all horses should be taking part.
He seems sincere, but bear in mind, of course,
even if he is not a horse at heart
that doesn't mean he's not, in fact, a horse,

though given all the medals he could win
being a horse, it's odd that he would choose
not to be one. You ought to see him grin
when he pulls off his semi-circle shoes.

Glass Eyebrow

the end   an eyebrow   where I draw the line
glass eyebrow   I occasionally raise
for company   only the Shugborough sign
only an eyebrow misses you   bouquets

The Shugborough sign has seen me go South East,
has seen me head South West and to the coast.
The Shugborough sign has seen me as the least
important person, seen me as the most
and on some trips I turn to it and boast.

the end an eyebrow where I draw the line

Some people never see the Shugborough sign.
They pass it half asleep or in a daze.
No one has claimed it so it must be mine
glass eyebrow I occasionally raise
glass eyebrows on selected motorways.

Drivers have hurtled past the white and brown
Shugborough sign and passengers have dozed,
while I have passed the A-road to your town,
many a time, pretending it was closed

or not a possibility   my head
that it went wrong   for which I do not blame
the motorways   for even though they led
to you   may lead to better things   the same

Negotiate the fairest deal you can
although it might mean pulling punks from trees.
Those of us searching for a Shugborough man
request a motorway extension, please.

So bless so bless the Shugborough sign and praise
even the signs you may not understand.
You see them by the sides of motorways
but can't imagine what they might have planned:

a parrot as a substitute for words,
a festival assistant with a sneer
fluttering slowly to a world of birds.
The Shugborough man has missed another year,

but he is coming just as you were not,
and meanwhile life goes on and plastic trays
bring all-day brunches and the weather's hot

only an eyebrow misses you   bouquets

Four Short Poems

THE MIND I LOSE

Whether the things I feel are true
or just illusion on my part,
I think that I'm in love with you
and wouldn't want to doubt my heart.

You say my heart may not exist.
I know it does, but isn't what
I once believed. This adds a twist,
the like of which can save a plot.

Feelings and thoughts are kept apart
unfairly by the words we choose.
Find me a better name than heart
by which to call the mind I lose.

BREAK THE COMPASS

To love him would be inconvenient.
My helpful friends are making out a list
of how my spare time might be better spent,
ironing clothes and towels – I get the gist,
but if he needs a pen-knife or a tent
that I can put discreetly in his hands,
if I'm the only one who can prevent
the dereliction of his little lands
then I will strike the talking oblongs dumb
and break the compass if they try to steer
my thoughts away from him, and they'll become
the inconvenience they claim to fear.

TO WISH ON YOU

You left a yellow imprint on my eye
which I'll remember longer than your face.
In a dark room with roof like winter sky
you were the only star to light the place.

You stood beneath the spotlight and you shone
while its strong beams fell down on you and then
you stepped away and all the shine was gone.
I'm waiting here for you to shine again.

Convince this audience that you belong
up there in dark or light and I will try
to wish on you but only for as long
as there's a yellow imprint on my eye.

Somebody else is sitting in your chair,
doing the same thing you did, just the same,
except he isn't you. His build, his hair –
both lighter, and he has a longer name

so now the wages book looks different, signed.
His tapes are where your bike-lights used to be,
next to the floppy disc tray, just behind
your mug (now his) which still says, 'I love tea'.

He doesn't though. Sometimes I catch his eye
and wonder if I'll find him gone one day
or if he'll see a different face at my
desk in due course. But he just looks away.

She Can Win Favour

Her friend the locksmith readily believes
the tales she tells of all the locks she's picked.
She can win favour with a gang of thieves
by itemising all the goods she's nicked,
and then you hear her talking to a judge
about the many crimes she has prevented.
Confectioners are told she's fond of fudge,
landlords, about the properties she's rented.
She can be just like anyone she meets
by flicking through her catalogue of poses –
ally of underdogs and of élites,
to gardeners she boasts of pruning roses,
to firemen of the time she braved the fire –
never to liars, though, that she's a liar.

Ms Quicksand is a Bitch

Reflected personality –
defence and favoured myth
of Mrs Smith, whose treachery
is loved by Mr Smith.

Husband is nice so wife must be
when right beside the moans
of Mrs Jones, what do you see?
The smile of Mr Jones.

Mrs Brown's shoes have heavy soles
for treading people down
while badgers, dolphins, bears and moles
are saved by Mr Brown.

When Mrs House (née Flat) agreed
to marry Mr House
she must have known that she would need
a mitigating spouse

but would he live with, sleep with, stay
with, would he share a bed…?
Yes, and you see it every day,
the wed, the not yet wed –

If mountaintops were not too high
to recognise a ditch,
then Mr Hill would not deny
Ms Quicksand is a bitch.

Running into Late

Where is the taxi's plastic pyramid?
Wasting another evening in the shed.
The case you carry never does or did
succeed in putting motives in your head.
Nobody has enough of anything,
nor will they find it underneath the lid
of some enamelled box, coiled in a spring

in the settee that festers on the ranch,
which was where I used to balance my peanut butter,
or in the tree you study branch by branch
or in the stadium or in the gutter.
You talk of nature and the man-made world
but miss the boot-sale and the avalanche.
Hair that alternately is crimped and curled

(if hair is not enough, what hope has skin?)
has not been known to drag you from the screen,
and is your bottle really worth the spin
if punts and parents jointly intervene?
Is God distinguished from the latest cult?
Not if you run your life by maximin:
aim for the least obnoxious worst result.

My main objection isn't that you wait
but that impatience would achieve far more.
If early wasn't running into late
I could respect the things you waited for.
Meanwhile I must conclude you're not the one,
watching you lift the packing from the crate,
looking for relics of ancestral fun.

The Downfall of Her Oscillating Head

After he called her idol nondescript
both what she felt and who she felt it for
became a pool of oil from which she slipped
into a strange illusion of the law.

On paper headed *this peculiar thing*,
the summons that he found beside his bed
charged him with rigid air conditioning,
the downfall of her oscillating head.

With strictly rehabilitative zest
all traces of him vanished from the lease
to relocate, entirely for the best,
on a mosaic patio in Greece

where his bread rolls were filled with Feta cheese
and round machines on rubber tubes inhaled
the insects from his bath – how to appease
spikes on which one was recently impaled.

Back home, the sensors he installed detect
that she is eating popcorn by the fire,
wondering how a sane man can respect
the form above the content of desire.

He leaves his business card on several boats.
His name is linked to some obscure mistake
while, in a jogging suit, the idol floats
off in a wicker basket down the lake

and doesn't ring but makes the same joke twice
about the things he hasn't done for years.
His fading mouth declares it might be nice.
Lords are behind it when he disappears.

Two Poems about Music

commissioned for the 1995 Huddersfield Contemporary Music Festival

HER KIND OF MUSIC

Her kind of music was a song
About a broken heart,
While his was complicated, long,
And labelled 'modern art'

With links to the chromatic scale.
The opera he wrote,
To her ears, was a lengthy wail
Upon a single note.

She struggled to acquire his taste
(As frequently occurs),
While, with enthusiastic haste,
He did away with hers.

WHEN A POET LOVES A COMPOSER

One look at him and I forgot,
Embarrassingly soon,
That music ought to have, if not
Lyrics, at least a tune.

He's highbrow in a big, big way
But when he sees that I'm
The one, he'll think that it's okay
For poetry to rhyme.

Soft-Handed Man

She couldn't love a man who had soft hands
and didn't do constructive things with wood,
but if she met one that she loved, she could.
She's right to say we all make strange demands
and right to think that no one understands.
Hard hands are not indicative of good

character, don't infallibly belong
to rugged, silent types who rarely shave,
who are, in equal measures, kind and brave.
Just over the horizon there's a strong
soft-handed man waiting to prove her wrong,
and when a person proves you wrong, they save

acres of mind you were about to close
and turn it into habitable land.
Each time you hold an unexpected hand
and stare at features that you never chose,
you're dealing with authority that knows
better than you how well things can be planned.

Selling His Soul

When someone says they have a poet's soul
You can imagine laughing in their face –
A sensible reaction on the whole
But he convinced me that it was the case
And that his poet's soul was out of place
What with his body selling advertising space.

The easy explanations sprang to mind –
Was he pretentious, arrogant, insane,
Or was it possible he'd been assigned
just what he said, and that his poet's brain,
Like a Laguna in the left hand lane,
Found itself trapped on unfamiliar terrain?

Even if there was just a one-in-five
Chance of it being true, I'd take the bet;
The souls of advertising salesmen thrive
In many of the poets I have met,
And if I'm right to think I won't forget
His soul, he's passed the best test anyone could set.

His life was going to change. He felt inspired,
He said, and vanished from my line of sight.
I didn't follow him. I have admired
The way Lagunas fly past on the right
While slower cars can only watch their flight,
Stuck in a ten mile tailback, every foggy night.

Double That Amount

for my car

It's not the money I will have to pay
To Nixon's Garage for the odd new part –
I would put double that amount their way
If they could beat the panels of my heart
Back to their happy shape before the dent
To your rear door. That would be cash well spent.

Now all my friends are trying to explain
What, in the land of logic, may be true:
That cars don't suffer. Cars do not feel pain.
I believe this like most car owners do
Yet can imagine how you're going to feel
For all the time it takes your door to heal.

This time next week, you'll be as good as new
But time is not the comfort that we need
Since I can wish it forwards (backwards too)
But can't change its direction or its speed,
Can't flip to either after or before
The damage to your injured, dented door.

As good as new, though – that means nothing lost
Apart from money, more of which I'll make
And your repairs, however much they cost
Are cheap to me. Money for money's sake
Is worthless in my mind, where feelings count
For everything and double that amount.

Ticket to Staines

I'd emerged from the second of two freezing trains
With a bag full of cheese salad sandwich remains
When I met a tree surgeon who said he was broke
And asked me to buy him a ticket to Staines.

He told me a jumbled, unfortunate tale
About how he had broken the terms of his bail
And he had to get back to his Mum's before ten
Or the cops would be taking him straight back to jail.

He told me his story outside Euston station
Describing his crime and its justification:
His tree surgeon's chainsaw had sliced through a train
In an effort to sabotage veal transportation.

His Mum had lumbago and no credit card
For a telephone booking. I thought long and hard
And it seemed to be me and me only that stood
Between him and a grilling at New Scotland Yard.

With diminishing faith in the state of my brains
And without quite condoning the slicing of trains
I led him past Knickerbox, Sock Shop and all
And bought that tree surgeon a ticket to Staines.

What will become of him? Where will he go?
(And don't say, 'You paid for it, you ought to know.')
I mean, is there a place for him? Is there a place
For a lawbreaking tree surgeon, chainsaw in tow?

There's a place for the tyrant who rules and constrains,
For the person who keeps other people in chains.
Wherever that tree surgeon goes, freedom reigns.
I wish I could see him arriving in Staines.

Postcard from a Travel Snob

I do not wish that anyone were here.
This place is not a holiday resort
with karaoke nights and pints of beer
for drunken tourist types – perish the thought.

This is a peaceful place, untouched by man –
not like your seaside-town-consumer-hell.
I'm sleeping in a local farmer's van –
it's great. There's not a guest house or hotel

within a hundred miles. Nobody speaks
English (apart from me and rest assured,
I'm not your sun-and-sangria-two-weeks
small-minded-package-philistine-abroad).

When you're as multi-cultural as me,
your friends become wine connoisseurs, not drunks.
I'm not a British tourist in the sea;
I am an anthropologist in trunks.

His Rising

They say it started with the climbing frame
his parents bought him when he was a boy.
They say that he was never quite the same,
that he progressed from climbing frame to trees,
            wanting a bigger toy.
They say now there is nothing that he sees,
nothing protruding that he won't ascend.
When he looks down, people the size of fleas
seem unimpressive from his higher perch;
            to recognise a friend
would mean binoculars, a pointless search.

His bride-to-be, a tiny dot below,
whom he would marry just to climb the church,
can stare up pipes until her neck is sore
        but she will never know
who or what kept him on the ground before,
what he now feels the need to rise above.
They say the only way we can endure
his rising and resist the urge to sink
        is with our minds off love.
Our mode of elevation is to think
about the closeness needed for a war.

Loss Adjuster

Scale down your expectations once again
from rest of life to years to one whole night
to will he wander past a phone or pen.
If he would only either ring or write.
Get real and scale those expectations down
from conversation to a single word –
seen through the window of a shop in town
if not by you then by a trusted third
party, or, if a sighting is too much
to hope for (as undoubtedly it is)
scale down your hopes and aim to see or touch
someone whose name sounds similar to his.
A scale of one to ten. Two weeks ago
he dared to keep you waiting while he slept.
Scale down much further and today's poor show
tomorrow you'll be happy to accept.

Two Hundred and Sixty-Five Words

I know exactly what I want to say.
I've estimated how long it will take.
I've weighed the trouble that will come my way
Against the difference saying it could make
And with no help from the mysterious They
Who ought to fight for people's right to speak,
I use my word allowance for today,
My conversation ration for the week

To talk about the baby with no manger,
The gold, myrrh, frankincense he never got,
Who was brought up for profit by a stranger
And invoiced for a rattle and a cot.
His rattle was the one thing he was fond of.
No time to say what matters most to me
Before I'm heard, before they snap the wand of
The upstart fairy on the Christmas tree.

She over-waved that wand. She used to wave it
At all bad things, hoping to make them good.
Who confiscated it? Who, later, gave it
Back to her as a heap of broken wood?
Call now with some inane response or other.
There are two phones, a black one and a white.
The right one will connect you with your brother;
The wrong one and your brother died last night.

Soon I might say *Ninety-five pounds. Nice weather,*
And call you by a name that's not your own.
You think they might put two and two together.
Sound old, sound boring and hang up the phone.
You think if we speak out then they can't touch us,
The Indiscriminately-Known-As-They
Who are responsible. Well, in as much as
I'm one of them, wave all your wands this way.

I'll Give Him This

The clothes he irons either burn or drown
And he wears tennis shoes to scale a cliff.
I doubt that he could name two shops in town
But he can tell a Rizla from a riff.
I'll give him this: the man can really roll a spliff.

He fears asparagus and foods with shells.
He can make heavy inroads overnight
Into your stock of Boddingtons and Bells.
That's a great song, he'll say, and he'll be right,
Rolling a spliff that's not too loose and not too tight.

He wouldn't know a saucer from a cup
But he can talk about election polls
While strumming his guitar or skinning up.
He loses small things like remote controls
But find fault with the songs he loves, the joints he rolls.

He's never dabbled in nouvelle cuisine
Or dazzled with a literary joke.
Don't tell me how inadequate he's been
At parties; if the guests don't sing or smoke,
If it's some vol-au-vent affair, he's not your bloke

But if you like tobacco on your rug
And if you want to watch a work of art
Emerging from a soft, illegal drug
His resurrection brain, his cowboy heart
Are highly recommended as a place to start.

My Enemies

My enemies, polished inside their caskets
My enemies sparkle behind glass doors
My enemies, curled into tilted baskets
My enemies, not yours

my enemies   You cannot steal or hire them
my enemies   You cannot loan or share
my enemies   Don't tidy or admire them
Don't even see them there

my enemies   Steer clear of the display case
My enemies try to make false amends
my enemies   The pallor of your grey face
will make them shine like friends

My enemies, proud of their faults and failings
my enemies   You take them out for tea
My enemies, beckoning through the railings
at a novice enemy

My enemies will give you proper training
My enemies shuffle up shelves for you
my enemies   The old ones are complaining
I like them better new

my   a new enemy   an equidistant
enemy showing every friend the door
politely, like a personal assistant
my enemies   One more

The Subject and the Object

Where injuries undress behind a screen
there is a way round saying what you mean.
The most decisive firebomb will assume
        the profile of a
ladder at the window of a burning room.

No sooner is your loft secured with string –
listen – the cellar crowns another King
with whom there is no time to disagree,
        so subtle that he
spells the word revenge without the letter 'v',

in deference to whom fish take the bones
out of themselves. Peaches emit their stones.
This King is an unusual event.
        You'd think a cat was
purring when his subjects came to pay the rent.

I'll give up words like 'troublesome' and 'hard'
and buy some skin cream for his business card.
One half that calculates, one half that cares –
        our combination
King, the best thing we have ever had downstairs,

attributing the days he saves to Spring,
and to the wind the tearing off of string.
He takes no credit and his voice is soft
        when he assures you
all you hear is cries of birds above the loft.

What You Deserve

I could pay you a fortune;
alternatively
I could ask for a fortune
and you could pay me.

I could tell you true stories
and false ones as well
but they all would be stories
I'd rather not tell.

I can live without justice,
at least live without
any version of justice
I might bring about,

for if my contribution
was wounds in the fight
shouldn't your contribution
be putting it right?

I have built no defences
nor will I attack
someone else's defences;
I'll get my own back

without blackmail or violence,
which call for less nerve
than to wait in long silence
for what you deserve.

All Wrong for Some

The cutlery is starting to annoy you.
It's either ladles or it's slotted spoons.
Early and late conspire to destroy you.
If it's not mornings then it's afternoons.
Both are containers clearly marked *conniption*.
Both are sufficient cause to be irate.
Mornings are not part of your job description,
Neither are afternoons. Early and late –
The way they start apart, then club together
To form a day, the way those footsteps crunch
Along the gravel path, along your tether
Right to the end. You blame it all on lunch,
For linking what should not be linked, for spawning
An afternoon as worthless as the morning.

You spend it looking forward to it ending
But when it ends, something is still not right:
You realise you can't go on pretending
That day is more unpopular than night
Or Winter more unpopular than Summer.
You blame the Springs and Autumns in between.
Boring old season, seasonal newcomer –
Neither is green enough, both are too green.
Enough to turn your masterpiece to stencils.
You wave your paintbrush at the scary face.
Paint starts to run. If you had stuck to pencils
That grey self-portrait would have known its place.
Now, when you look at it inside its frame, you
See that you hate yourself, and who can blame you.

Nod and Smile

'You couldn't take him anywhere,' she said,
'Even your best friends wouldn't want to know.'
She must have thought I harboured in my head
A glossy guide to places we could go.

'There's nowhere I could take him,' I agree.
She takes the opportunity to breathe a
Sigh of relief, then she turns back to me
And says, 'He'd never let you leave him either.'

'I couldn't ever leave him,' I concede.
There's much agreement in our brief exchange.
She's thrilled and I am not, but we're agreed
That circumstances won't improve or change,

That I could save myself a lot of pain.
There's not a word she says I don't believe –
Much easier only to entertain
Thoughts of a person you can take, or leave.

Pink and the Gang

Pink house in a grey town,
Thin house on a long street,
White stone house and brown –
All raise their rents to beat

The house that won't compete –
The tall house by the sea
Who says, to cries of cheat,
Do not charge rent for me.

However loud his voice
They'll make their rents as large.
They will be seen as choice;
He, as ashamed to charge.

White, brown, pink and thin
Monopolise the streets.
Materialists move in,
Are rewarded with receipts

While the tall sea house takes
Nothing but love and thanks
From his tenant, who mistakes
Pink and the gang for banks.

The Man Who Wouldn't Share His Garden with a Wolf

I try to keep my cool –
difficult when the thieving
bastard has got his paws inside my pool,
tail on my grass, and shows no sign of leaving.
I don't know what the fool
thinks he's achieving.

He calls himself my friend.
The place, he calls exquisite.
Creep. Just a while, he said. So, to extend
that while to permanence is friendly, is it?
A visit with no end
is not a visit.

Which would be more unkind,
to draw a line, restrict him
to one half of the garden, or to find
a pretext upon which I could evict him?
To have him off my mind,
even inflict him

on somebody I hate –
one of the grin and bear it
brigade, who almost pushed him through my gate,
who now sit back and murmur how unfair it
is for a man of great
wealth not to share it.

Good guilt-inducing trick,
but false, since I would harden
my heart, if I was poor, over a brick.
You heard me. Never mind I beg your pardon.
Get the ungrateful prick
out of my garden.

Liberation Day

My tunnel wasn't yet complete.
I shook from heavy earrings
New dust each day around my feet
In muddy forest clearings.

The aperture was well concealed,
My tools were safe and polished
When a news bulletin revealed
Walls were to be demolished.

I have shed large amounts of sweat,
I've crawled and cried and shivered
And now I hear we're going to get
Deliverance delivered.

I am not over-keen to bleed,
I didn't take to scraping
But it is one thing being freed,
Another thing escaping.

Digging has helped me through the day,
Digging has made me stronger.
I can't, with nothing in the way,
Make my short tunnel longer.

I will sit centre stage, front row
And clap as each brick tumbles
But where will my half-tunnel go
If the whole building crumbles?

I'll wait for Liberation Day.
The roof will lift, the sun'll
shine and with new, free speech I'll say
I want to build my tunnel.

In Layman's Terms

If he wants proof, he only has to ask.
Let him admit to disbelief and doubt.
Tell him that I am equal to the task
Of driving all his reservations out
And if he sees no face behind the mask,
Where is the faith I've heard so much about?

If he wants proof, he had his proof before.
I could provide a bibliography.
He doesn't think I know him anymore;
I've mixed him up with what he used to be.
I also may have changed and yet he's sure
That he addresses his remarks to me.

Our words connect the present to the past
Each time we speak, simply by making sense.
So tell him this, the next time doubt is cast:
The risks I take are at my own expense.
If he has faith then he should be the last
To give up hope, despite the evidence;

A standpoint known as love, in layman's terms,
Namely determination to succeed
Though odds are stacked and though suspicion worms
Its way through hearts and nothing's guaranteed.
No fact disproves all this and none confirms
And if he still needs proof, he'll have to need.

The Good Loser

I have portrayed temptation as amusing.
Now he can either waver or abstain.
His is a superior kind of losing
And mine is an inferior brand of gain.

His sacrifice, his self-imposed restriction
Will get through this controversy intact
For his is a superior kind of fiction
And mine is an inferior brand of fact.

I have displayed my most attractive feature
And he his least, yet still the match seems odd.
For I am a superior kind of creature
And he is an inferior brand of god

And if he cuts me off without a warning
His is the book from which I'll take a leaf
For his is a superior kind of mourning
And ours a most inferior brand of grief.

A Strong Black Coffee for the Sleeping Dog

They let you in. You interrupt their dinner.
You're on your back instead of on your knees.
If you behave yourself, one day you'll win a
Glimpse of your loved one's chips and mushy peas.
           What do I have to do to be a sinner?
           Turn a saint's pencil forty-five degrees.

He had a small square yard for us to smoke in,
Behind a hut and safe from parish spies.
The room his parents used to put strange folk in
Was also square and of a matching size.
           I listened to the same twelve songs and spoke in
           The hushed tones of a consolation prize.

Perhaps I wasn't any consolation.
Perhaps he didn't want to be consoled.
Years ago, when he had an explanation
And would have told me, I would not be told.
           I hang around the graveyard and the station,
           Outside the dog-eared college, feeling old,

And glamorise the benches and the matches.
I put the faces back inside the room.
His jacket with the shiny shoulder patches –
Does he still have it and, if not, to whom
           Does it belong? One drops, another catches.
           One has a spade and plenty to exhume.

By now you will be guessing my agenda,
That I am here for reasons of my own,
Not being shy or wise enough to send a
Token or two then leave you all alone.
           I'm here in what should be my place, to spend a
           Day with a gentleman I should have known.

Since neither of the heartless queens is present,
I have become a princess not a frog
As far as he's concerned, but what bland, pleasant
Creature might he be stalking through the fog?
        I've got a croissant shaped just like a crescent,
        A strong black coffee for the sleeping dog.

I've come to demonstrate that to be able
Is what counts most. Too late and not too late
Have been defined today, and though unstable
Has given way to steady, mad to great,
        If he still keeps those objects on his table,
        There is a sort of chance, at any rate.

Sleep Well

He shook the feeling back into his arm
when its strange numbness woke him with a cry.
His wobbly leg caused only slight alarm
before connecting with its blood supply.

It's one thing, ladies, gentlemen, to wake
as did the man described above, like him
to feel dead digits, and to shake and shake
for a reunion with whichever limb

but in the early hours, with a start,
do not, like him, wake as an empty sack.
That man slept wrongly on his head and heart
and he will never get the feeling back.

Leaving and Leaving You

I

Occupational Hazard

He has slept with accountants and brokers,
With a cowgirl (well, someone from Healds).
He has slept with non-smokers and smokers
In commercial and cultural fields.

He has slept with book-keepers, book-binders,
Slept with auditors, florists, PAs,
Child psychologists, even child minders,
With directors of firms and of plays.

He has slept with the stupid and clever.
He has slept with the rich and the poor
But he sadly admits that he's never
Slept with a poet before.

Real poets are rare, he confesses,
While it's easy to find a cashier.
So I give him some poets' addresses
And consider a change of career.

This Morning in a Black Jag

In this ringroad-and-roundabout business park of a place,
Where the favourite phrases are modem and user-base
And a poet is probably seen as a waste of space,
I'm in need of a mode of transport and a familiar face

And I seem to have picked up a car with a man that drives –
Whenever I order a cab, it is he who arrives,
Drops me off at my nines and collects me from my fives,
And although for the bulk of the days we lead totally separate lives,

When I mentioned some places up north, he knew where they were,
And he even conceded Oasis were better than Blur,
And Jim Morrison blares from his cab, though he says he'd prefer
To be thought of not as a taxi driver but as a chauffeur.

To prove it, he turned up this morning in a black Jag,
And, while teaching bored youths how to write is no less of a drag
(You're explaining the sonnet, they're planning which lessons to wag),
It's more bearable when you turn up in a car about which you can brag.

Stroppy kids can't depress me – I'm lucky enough to have found
A man who leaves every day free just to drive me around,
Who asks how it went and who tells me which schools are renowned
For reducing the squeamish to tears. We have covered a fair bit
                                                    of ground

And we secretly wonder (we're both too polite to enquire)
Why his fares are much lower these days, why my tips are much higher,
Why our journeys get longer each time, so we tend to go via
This diversion or that, both pretending there's scenery there to admire.

For our last trip, he charges me half the original quote:
Just two pounds, but he gets the change from my five pound note
And I get the smell of his Jaguar on my coat
And a train journey home to read and re-read the receipts he wrote.

Your Dad Did What?

Where they have been, if they have been away,
or what they've done at home, if they have not –
you make them write about the holiday.
One writes *My Dad did*. What? Your Dad did what?

That's not a sentence. Never mind the bell.
We stay behind until the work is done.
You count their words (you who can count and spell);
all the assignments are complete bar one

and though this boy seems bright, that one is his.
He says he's finished, doesn't want to add
anything, hands it in just as it is.
No change. *My Dad did*. What? What did his Dad?

You find the 'E' you gave him as you sort
through reams of what this girl did, what that lad did,
and read the line again, just one 'e' short:
This holiday was horrible. My Dad did.

His First If Lady Only Just

I am the country of his fame;
his constitution knows I am.
With half a presidential name
he's my no-Lincoln Abraham.

Now that's a bit below the belt
he says, when relevant, to show
that while he ain't no Roosevelt
he's no mean Franklin Delano.

I throw his party left and right
and, like a Herbert chases dust,
I chase him all around the White,
his First if Lady only just.

I blow his mind but not his brains –
half-presidents are safe, I guess.
No Johnson but a Lyndon Baines,
a truer man than Harry S.

I am the country of his fame,
the Nancy who creates the Ron,
the one he's bound to shoot or frame
when all the love has pentagon.

Rondeau Redoublé

He likes the soup but doesn't like the spoon.
We hold opposing views on means and ends.
It's funny now, but it would matter soon
If we shared more than chinese food and friends.

In case he breaks the only time he bends,
He drinks the coffee, leaves the macaroon.
He says, as though pure anarchy descends,
He likes the soup but doesn't like the spoon.

I've sat in restaurants all afternoon,
Fallen for all the culinary trends
But to admit this seems inopportune.
We hold opposing views on means and ends.

Normally I am someone who defends
High living, but I let him call the tune
During these strange, occasional weekends.
It's funny now, but it would matter soon;

The earth won't sprout a ladder to the moon
Though we make compromises and amends.
It would be like December next to June
If we shared more than chinese food and friends.

Sometimes we clash, sometimes our difference blends
And the cold air turns hot in the balloon.
I tell myself (in case success depends
On attitude) that though he hates the spoon,
He likes the soup.

The Yellow and the Blue

Could be an armband or a rubber ring,
a lilo or a surfboard or a boat,
a wave (it needn't be a man-made thing)
that makes it briefly possible to float;
could be the lotion I slap on, rub in
to give the sun the temper of the shade,
or the umbrella that relieves my skin
while others turn to leather and to suede;
could be that in the pool or on the beach,
could be that in the yellow and the blue,
the tourist's miracles within my reach
are not commissioned or inspired by you,
and if to me you're block, board, ring and band
I am, as much as this is not, your land.

Against Road-building

He hated roads. He loved the land.
He tended to forget
Or else he didn't understand
That roads were how we met.

He loved long walks. He hated cars.
He often put them down.
Without them, though, I'd have reached Mars
Before I reached his town.

Now that I've seen bad air pervade
An atmosphere once sweet
I wish the car was never made
That drove me to his street.

Now that I've felt a world explode
As I had not before
I wish they'd never built the road
That led me to his door.

None of the Blood

None of the blood that is in your body
   is in my body. None of the blood
      that is in my body is in your body.
Whatever you are, you are not my blood.

None of the flesh that is on your body
   is on my body. None of the flesh
      that is on my body is on your body.
Whatever you are, you are not my flesh.

I have shared a bottle of wine with a bigot
   (none of the eggshells, none of the mud
      in my kitchen and garden, your kitchen and garden).
None of the flesh. None of the blood

that is in my kitchen is in your kitchen.
   (I am being rude. I am not just being rude.)
      None of your garden is in my garden.
I have shared a picnic bench with a prude.

Furniture, yes, means of transport, yes,
   but no to soul and no to bone
      (none of your sellotape, none of your glue).
Yes to some stranger. No to you.

Marrying the Ugly Millionaire

Here comes my mother carrying
Dried flowers for my hair.
This afternoon I'm marrying
The ugly millionaire.

Here is my sister with the veil.
Everyone wants to share
My lucrative unholy grail –
The ugly millionaire.

There are our presents, wrapped and tied.
Soon they will fill the room.
All marked (no mention of the bride)
Attention of the groom –

No Dior, no St Laurent, no frills,
No full Le Creuset set.
Only my father's unpaid bills,
My brother's gambling debt,

Demands beyond and way above
What would be right or fair.
I hate the grasping lot. I love
The ugly millionaire.

The Wise One

I could not scrub the lift shaft with a toothbrush,
Spare time to stitch new bookmarks out of lace
Or carry boxes up and down rope ladders.
I'm not the helpful one around this place.
The helpful one is over there with a chipped marble face.

I will not press a calculator's buttons,
Clock in, tot up, give coins as change from notes.
I'm not the numbers one. Haven't they told you
How dizzy I am from counting last year's votes?
The numbers one is on the slab, under a pile of coats.

Don't come to me for vases of carnations –
I'd barely know a cactus from a rose.
Consult the experts for the best arrangements,
Flowery ones. I am not one of those.
The flowery one is in the earth, with everything that grows.

I haven't seen the overhead projector
This week. I cannot just nip down the road.
I'm not the knowing one, I'm not the going one,
Or the finding one. Those three are being towed
To a farm to be written out of a crucial episode.

Which one am I? I must be one. Everyone else is.
Look at those little pet other ones, shining their knees,
No doubts as to which ones they are. Which one am I?
The answering one, the resolving one? Neither of these.
Try the wise one, the free one, but only if everyone else agrees.

Ruining the Volunteer

I'm ruining the volunteer today.
I get through sometimes nine or ten a year,
Or even more, if more are sent my way.
Today I'm ruining the volunteer.

I first suggest he asks for decent wages,
More than his measly travel reimbursed.
We're still in the preliminary stages.
It's always worth suggesting wages first.

The volunteer denies he's on the breadline
Because thus far he's had his bread with jam.
He practises liasing with a deadline
As if my sound advice weren't worth a damn.

He'll learn at his expense for his expenses.
Tomorrow, volunteer, you'll be assailed
By demonstrations of what common sense is
And words you never use, words like curtailed,

Buffeted, buttressed, bulwark, bolstered, bounded –
Powerful words with plenty to express.
Tomorrow, volunteer, you'll be surrounded
By those who wouldn't leave their beds for less.

So pick me up at six in my pyjamas,
Put on my gloves and coat, pull up my hood.
This is how postmen feel, postmen and farmers.
Oh, stop complaining. It will do you good

Or put you off. I hinder and delay you
For your own good. For mine, you leap ahead.
I'm neither able nor inclined to pay you.
Volunteer, I cannot get out of bed.

Four Sonnets

UNSAVOURY (COULD ALMOST PASS FOR SWEET)

He parks where he is not allowed to park
and does what he is ill-advised to do.
As reassuring as a question mark,
his words are neither sensible nor true
but still I let him know that he's preferred.
His nod confirms that he can be discreet.
The way he twists the meaning of a word
unsavoury could almost pass for sweet.

Sweet: in my weaker moments, everyone
rallies around and soon I have a list
of twenty reasons why I ought to run.
My reason is the only one they've missed:
not all the bad things he may do or be
but that he's better at them all than me.

NEVER HIS

I freeze as I'm about to write his name.
Politely, he reminds me who he is.
What can I say that won't sound trite or lame –
I could forget some names, but never his?
So I say nothing, simply write it down,
hand him the envelope and let him leave,
though I'm inclined to chase him all round town
to put this right, tamper with clocks, retrieve
the eyes that wavered and the hand that shook,
the hesitation he perceived as tact,
the blush he understandably mistook
for loss of memory (which now, in fact,
is sharper than it was, and will replay
him telling me his name all night, all day).

TYPECASTING

Not knowing you, I thought I knew your type –
how you'd behave, the sort of thing you'd say.
I guessed you'd be inclined to take a swipe
at anybody getting in your way.
I told my friends you were like this, like that,
had you evading taxes, cutting throats,
gave you a line in patronising chat,
presented my imaginings as quotes.
But your behaviour is exemplary.
Your words have been, without exception, kind.
Do you have preconceived ideas of me?
If I am not yet typecast in your mind,
can I suggest the fool who will insist
on putting words in mouths she should have kissed?

SOMETHING INVOLVING US

I was so drunk, I don't remember much –
not how your body felt and not your arms
around me, not your dinner-suited touch
between two cars (not setting off alarms).
I do remember, though, the next day's drink,
your calmness, your I-still-respect-you smile,
and I remember that you said, 'I think
it's better if we leave it for a while.'
I next remember that you changed your mind,
and changed your mind, and changed your mind again,
as if, for you, something remained behind
(something I missed, not being sober then)
from that first night, something involving us,
that makes what's happened since seem worth the fuss.

Diminishing Returns

I will tell outright lies where you embellish.
Your yawn will be my cue to fall asleep.
Anyone who is watching us with relish
Will find that, where your talk and tricks are cheap,
Mine will be cast-offs. When you stop at kissing
I'll stop at shaking hands; you eye the clock,
I'll grab my watch and gasp at what I'm missing
And any door you close, I'll double-lock.
Operate slowly – I'll stand still for ever.
Leave quickly – I will be the speed of light
Passing you on the way, and if we never
Do anything constructive, that's all right
(Though it will be a wasted chance) because
While casual observers say of you
'He led her on', of me they'll say, 'She was
The less enthusiastic of the two.'

This Calculating Field

A threatened field knows that it must give way
to a new road, starts to prepare for change,
turns, in anticipation, almost grey.
Everyone says *doesn't the grass look strange?*

The green that once inspired them to protest
has lost its charm, character, former fame.
Change can now safely be compared to rest.
The grass turns grey, ready to take the blame

as well as all effects of the assault.
Forget the luxury of looking good;
assume control. *Yes it is all my fault.*
If I did not turn bad, somebody would.

Can I have won and at the same time lost
all of my qualities that once appealed?
The outcome of a benefit and cost
equation is this calculating field

turning to grey. Your sadness in defending
becomes exhilaration in attack.
I can imagine only one good ending:
where you are glad that I will not be back.

Leaving and Leaving You

When I leave your postcode and your commuting station,
When I leave undone the things that we planned to do
You may feel you have been left by association
But there is leaving and there is leaving you.

When I leave your town and the club that you belong to,
When I leave without much warning or much regret
Remember, there's doing wrong and there's doing wrong to
You, which I'll never do and I haven't yet,

And when I have gone, remember that in weighing
Everything up, from love to a cheaper rent,
You were all the reasons I thought of staying
And you were none of the reasons why I went

And although I leave your sight and I leave your setting
And our separation is soon to be a fact,
Though you stand beside what I'm leaving and forgetting,
I'm not leaving you, not if motive makes the act.

A Division Fence

Dictate to me my house   you the more clever
the more aware   our past has consequences

      the purchaser's heirs and assigns will make and forever
      hereafter maintain a division fence or fences

whisper   *restrictive covenant*   whenever
they hover in the grounds   you the more gifted

      the purchaser's heirs and assigns will make and forever

whisper   *restrictive covenant unlifted*

whisper   *so heavy with the weight of lawyers*
my fence   *in stick three names together firms*
They hover in the grounds   weak wood destroyers
whisper   *strong wood*   *strong wood*   Dictate the terms

They are a slow man's marathon from harmless
What do we like? Clean and straightforward Deeds
here at the firm of Grudge Successful Charmless

oh let me let me let me in it pleads

misunderstanding   fence *neurotic*   border
Stand firm   *fence*   *fence*   the firm of Brick Flesh Wood
No heir of mine and no assign to order
oh let you in   as if your Deeds were good

Next Door Despised

Next door despised
your city. They would much prefer a town.
Your tree – they'd like a twig.
Your oil rig,
your salmon satin crown,
so can you cut it down and cut it down?

Next door began
a harsh campaign. They hired a ticket tout
to sell your oily tree,
your haddocky
crown for a well of drought,
and then they bricked it up and shut it out.

Next door perceived
an envelope was lying on your stoop
but no one wrote to them
so your silk hem
deserved their mushroom soup.
Next door made plans to follow you to group

therapy, pinch
your problems, change their characters and looks.
Next door alleged your streams
gave them bad dreams.
Couldn't you call them brooks?
Couldn't you write some better, shorter books?

Next door observed
your shoulder stump, asked what was up your sleeve,
swore that they meant no harm,
said that to arm
dictators was naïve
(no pun intended). Next door don't believe

you've gone to work,
neither the place nor the activity.
While next door's squirrel slipped,
your manuscript
lolled on the balcony
which might seem natural to you or me

but to next door
it was a gate wide enough to admit
the dwarves in overcoats
who chase weak votes,
whose coffee smells of shit,
whose stubble shakes only when candle-lit.

Next door have got
their own house but they choose to squat in yours.
If you brought up their theft
of what was left
and asked whose ceilings, floors
and walls these were, next door would say next door's.

Barbecue!

I can afford to lose a window pane,
for once a month a brandy glass to break.
He is related to the hurricane.
I tolerate its visits for his sake.

Tracing his tree directly to the flood
we float a lot, but as he pointed out
we remain dry beside the running mud
courtesy of his ancestor the drought.

Our food is either ash or somehow scarred.
Barbecue! he announces, for the fire
is his relation too, one of the charred
tastes (or disasters) I must now acquire.

All this would matter if we'd met by chance
but I, for all his kinship to the quake,
spring from the siren and the ambulance.
One rumble and my foot comes off the brake.

Like Carnivals

I thought I saw you pass in the parade,
masked on a float or clapping in the crowd,
and was persuaded by the sense it made
that among many, one might be allowed

(one random body at the hotdog stand
or chance extension of the burger queue,
trombone or trumpet player in the band,
even a clown) to turn out to be you.

At all events where people congregate
like carnivals and festivals and balls
I seek our little world within the great,
turning horizons into bedroom walls.

The Burning Scheme

The newly burned are queuing in the shop,
leaf-fall-in-autumn jigsaws on their skin.
Everyone only wants the pain to stop
      as they survey the crop
of Delial, Ambre Solaire, Piz Buin.
There is no lotion for the burn within.

The newly dazed are tethered to a wink.
Left eyes stand guard while right eyes squint and seep.
Everything has been tried: pills, a hot drink,
      a cream containing zinc,
everything that is popular and cheap.
The burn within thrives on a good night's sleep.

Moon like an orange in a sea of gin,
apply your coolness to a burning dream.
Hat with a mess thereunder, lift your chin,
      lift all the teeth therein.
How do you fit into the burning scheme,
hat of the famous England cricket team?

The burn within makes no attempt to cheat.
Its pockets, so to speak, are free of sand.
Fairly it wins and squarely it can beat
      every burn caused by heat,
hops on a night flight home, keen to expand
in the wet climate of its native land.

She Has Established Title

She keeps the lies and popular support.
I take the condemnation and the truth.
I claim the chase; she has already caught.
Her permanence is balanced by my youth.
The afternoons are mine. She hogs the nights,
The public sphere encompassed by her rings.
She has established title. All the rights
Are hers. How fairly we divide these things.
Each of us has a quite substantial list
Of goodies, and I wouldn't choose to swap,
Like football cards, the knowledge I exist
For both the mortgage and the weekly shop,
My inventory for hers, if someone were
To ask, or wonder, what I might prefer.

The Bridging Line

If, as it now appears,
a second time can lean across the ditch,
retrieve, like a dropped stitch,
the first, long in arrears,
how badly I've misjudged the last five years;

potholes beside our past
I thought they were, when all the time they've been
linear, in between,
travelling (if not fast)
towards next time, back from next time to last.

Tonight's no precipice,
merely one station on the bridging line
where incidents combine,
kiss throws a rope to kiss,
last time connects to next, next time to this –

a better fairytale
than scattered breadcrumbs on the forest floor;
wind howls, rain starts to pour
and soon you've lost your trail.
The bridging line is like a polished rail

beneath our years of space
that I can almost rest my hand upon.
I clutch it now you're gone,
find it reflects your face,
find I believe the next five years will race

straightforwardly ahead
as five have raced straightforwardly behind.
The gaps are redefined.
I hold my breath and tread
the bridging line towards a waiting bed.

Your Darlings

You call some women Darling and they fall
predictably in love, but say the same
to others (brighter ones, perhaps) and all
it means, they say, is that you're scared you'll call
one woman by another woman's name.

I know you get around a bit (I ought
to know) but can't presume to guess your fears
or what proportion of your conquests thought
your Darlings were sincere, or if the sort
of woman who believes her hopes and ears

predominates over the doubting kind
in your portfolio, whether a lapse
in disbelief makes a believing mind,
the lucky owner waking up to find
her prospects changed (to brighter ones, perhaps).

Some hunt and hunt until they find a fake
behind what either was or sounded true.
Those who are anything like me will take
the best interpretation, maybe make
fools of themselves, but make the most of you.

His Bounceability on Knees

She wound the scarf tightly around her eyes
thinking that if she couldn't see at all
she might forget that such a thing as size
existed, and pretend he wasn't small
but all the scarf blocked out was half the light;
his stunted shape persisted through the gauze
and she still knew that he was half her height
despite their flat shoes and the level floors
and all that she had seen in him at first,
things like his bounceability on knees,
did nothing but contribute to her thirst
for what was out of reach, past clouds and trees,
when – far above the skull that she could feel
against her thigh – racing around her head
were visions of a large, departing heel
shaking the nearby woodland with its tread.

Over and Elm and I

Nothing to recommend your feet
except that when you put them down
on Market Hill or Benet Street
you make a better town

Nothing to recommend your stance
except that anywhere you stand
soaks up your presence to enhance
all the surrounding land

No evidence you are a cure
but that the envelope you sealed
and hand-delivered to my door
held a St Neots field

Nothing but that you seem to reach
beyond the space you occupy
so that in March and Waterbeach
Over and Elm and Eye

pillows store imprints of your face
surprised to learn that there's a head
whose contact with a pillowcase
can so improve a bed

You hailed a taxi at the lights
now every single cab that turns
onto East Road like yours ignites
Even the downpour burns

In its stone pot the stand-up clock
turns to a flower on its stem
The county's little stations rock
I feel like one of them

Once When the Wind Blew

Our purses and our fumes
distinguish us, the normals, drys and oilies
who scan the tablecloths in auction rooms,
churn up the paper doilies

to find a cleaner head,
phrenology's bald, ornamental scalps,
black virtues sprinkled and black vices spread
on curves as white as Alps.

If we abandoned hair,
if, in its place, we could contrive to grow
lists of our qualities, complete but fair,
best and worst points on show,

the pain that it would save,
the moves from double into separate beds.
Imagine they are coming to engrave,
tomorrow, all our heads

and now's the time to dump
all that we judge unfit for public view.
We're talking ink (an enigmatic bump
is always subject to

interpretation, doubt,
with how it feels depending on the hand).
I would far rather have it all spelled out,
easy to understand.

Would I have felt that twinge
of sadness if I'd seen the word *inert*,
once when the wind blew, underneath your fringe,
or been so badly hurt

if just above your ear
capacity to cause unhappiness…
I could extend this game and this idea
but heads do not confess

failings to clumps of hair,
nor leave them stranded when the hair is gone,
but I know yours and when we meet somewhere
I'm going to carve them on.

Hardly Dear

I wouldn't buy you from a car boot sale,
not if your mind had been reduced to clear,
though you were overpriced at half a year.
With your significance cut down to scale

I could afford you. If you soon turned stale
I could point out that you were hardly dear
and that I'd had my money's worth, or near.
I wouldn't buy you from a car boot sale,

you or a size five shoe or books in braille –
I have no use for them. Let the sincere
stall-holder smile and say *a snip, a mere
pittance* as though he flogged the holy grail,

the greatest bargain in this hemisphere
rather than just a load of useless gear.
He might succeed with some. With me he'd fail.
I wouldn't buy you from a car boot sale.

Nobody Said You Had to Come

Why did you come to this workshop if you didn't want to write?
I can think of at least ten other things you could have done tonight.
As for good soaps you could have watched, there were an easy three.
Nobody said you had to come and spend two hours with me.

You're happy to drink a cup of tea and eat a chocolate biscuit
But asked to write some poetry, you'd prefer not to risk it
So are you here by accident? Was it an oversight?
Why did you come to this workshop if you didn't want to write?

You tell me firmly several times, to check I've understood,
That nothing I can say or do could make your poems good.
I am an optimist but I agree the chance is slight,
So why did you come to this workshop if you didn't want to write?

Did a vindictive spouse propel you here against your will
When all you wanted was to stay at home and watch *The Bill*?
Why, when I mention poems, do your eyes pop out in fright
And why did you come to this workshop if you didn't want to write?

The sign says *Writing Poetry*, which, I feel, makes it plain
That poetry will be involved, will even be the main
Activity on offer. It's spelled out in black and white.
Why did you come to this workshop if you didn't want to write?

Let me point out I'm doing this for money not for fun.
I don't care if you write or not. You're not the only one
Who will greet nine o'clock with unequivocal delight
But why did you come to the workshop if you didn't want to write?

Most of you spell quite well, so it's unlikely you've misread
Poetry and concluded it was *Pottery* instead.
Would you become a pilot, then refuse to board the flight?
Why did you come to this workshop if you didn't want to write?

All right then, if I'm under a complete misapprehension
And if producing poetry was never your intention,
Write a short piece of prose explaining why you're here, in spite
Of having not a lot to say and no desire to write.

If People Disapprove of You...

Make being disapproved of your hobby.
Make being disapproved of your aim.
Devise new ways of scoring points
In the Being Disapproved Of Game.

Let them disapprove in their dozens.
Let them disapprove in their hordes.
You'll find that being disapproved of
Builds character, brings rewards

Just like any form of striving.
Don't be arrogant; don't coast
On your high disapproval rating.
Try to be disapproved of most.

At this point, if it's useful,
Draw a pie chart or a graph.
Show it to someone who disapproves.
When they disapprove, just laugh.

Count the emotions you provoke:
Anger, suspicion, shock.
One point for each of these and two
For every boat you rock.

Feel yourself warming to your task –
You do it bloody well.
At last you've found an area
In which you can excel.

Savour the thrill of risk without
The fear of getting caught.
Whether they sulk or scream or pout,
Enjoy your new-found sport.

Meanwhile, all those who disapprove
While you are having fun
Won't even know your game exists
So tell yourself you've won.

III

Tribute

For the first time I find it quite unnerving
That people's names are handed on to things.
No bench, so far, has proved itself deserving
Enough to bear your name. No hospice wings
Or students' union buildings will inherit,
If it has anything to do with me,
A name no other man could even merit
Let alone any slice of brick or tree.
I could be Lord Mayor with a town to listen
To my new street names; you would still be gone.
Now, as myself, with power to rechristen
No roads, there's still a tribute going on:
Though I call nothing by your name, I do
Practically nothing but call after you.

The League of Saints

The blister on my heel has healed.
Each day there's more between
This laundry and the lake and field,
What is and what has been,
Or, by the currents of our blood,
Me and a future queen.

Each day, each minute, hauls the mud
From the concealing mist
And strips the glamour from the dud,
Gauze from the fractured wrist
But I have soared too high in rank
For us to co-exist.

I thank all those I ought to thank
But I am in the place
Of every miracle that sank
With or without a trace.
As if all smiles were mine by right
I robbed a mouthless face.

Each seventh generation night
Revives the ankle sprain,
The sound of static and the slight
Psychosis of the rain.
The moss that issues from her slab
Furs my approaching train.

The blister on my heel's a scab.
I am no longer dressed
In swamp, or bleeding in a cab
Bound for a shrine South West
But lots of things were crushed and lost
When we became the best.

I could have easily been tossed,
Demented, in the lake,
As popular as an embossed
Horse mistress at the wake.
She and I share the strength to hoist
Our men above the rake

And I, and no doubt she, rejoiced
When it at last transpired
That all the prayers we'd rasped and voiced
And all the bombs we'd wired
Blew us towards the league of saints
We worshipped and admired.

The visors, boiler-suits and paints
All add to the effect.
Likewise if someone shrieks or faints,
Likewise if lives are wrecked
And silent in the music booth
The founder of our sect,

His schizophrenic glaze of youth.
Processional, we stalk.
Whether I'm closer to his truth
Than islands in New York,
The blister on my heel has healed.
Take up your shoe and walk.

Steven's Side

I am supporting Steven
as if I were a beam
      under his ceiling, even
though he is not a team.
      Under his ceiling even
a nightmare is a dream.

Steven and I have entered.
Some people have implied
      I would be too self-centred
to cheer for Steven's side,
      I would be too self-centred
to fail if Steven tried.

I am supporting Steven
as if I were a rail
      behind his curtain, even
though he is bound to fail.
      Behind his curtain even
a white net is a veil.

Steven is no performer.
He has no gift for sport.
      I make no cool crowd warmer
by staging my support.
      I make no cool crowd warmer,
adorn no tennis court

but I am supporting Steven
as if I were a pin
      above his hemline, even
though he will never win.
      Above his hemline even
a jacket is a skin.

I am supporting Steven.
I am at Steven's feet.
       I put him first and even
give him a thing to beat.
       I put him first and even
then he will not compete.

In Wokingham on Boxing Day
at The Edinburgh Woollen Mill

Two earnest customers compare
a ribbed and unribbed sleeve.
I wonder what I'm doing here
and think I ought to leave,
get in my car and drive away.
       I stand beside the till
       in Wokingham on Boxing Day
       at The Edinburgh Woollen Mill.

All of the other shops are closed.
Most people are in bed.
Somehow I know that I'm supposed
to find an A–Z.
Somehow I sense I must obey
       an unfamiliar will
       in Wokingham on Boxing Day
       at The Edinburgh Woollen Mill.

I parked in a disabled space
so either I'm a cheat
or a debilitating case
of searching for your street
has started to erode away
      my locomotive skill
      in Wokingham on Boxing Day
      at The Edinburgh Woollen Mill,

somewhere perhaps you've never been.
I doubt you're into wool.
Even if mohair's not your scene
the atmosphere is full
of your proximity. I sway
      and feel a little ill
      in Wokingham on Boxing Day
      at The Edinburgh Woollen Mill.

The sales assistants wish me luck
and say they hope I find
the place I want. I have been stuck
with what I left behind,
with what I've been too scared to say,
      too scared to say until
      in Wokingham on Boxing Day
      at The Edinburgh Woollen Mill

I tell myself the time is now;
willingly I confess
my love for you to some poor cow
in an angora dress
whose *get lost loony* eyes convey
      her interest, which is nil,
      in Wokingham on Boxing Day
      at The Edinburgh Woollen Mill.

I find your house. You're still in bed.
I leave my gift and flee,
pleased with myself, not having said
how you can contact me,
driven by fears I can't allay,
        dreams I did not fulfil
        in Wokingham on Boxing Day
        at The Edinburgh Woollen Mill.

Chains are the most distressing shops.
They crop up everywhere.
The point at which the likeness stops
squeezes my lungs of air.
When I see jumpers on display
        I wish that I was still
        in Wokingham on Boxing Day
        at The Edinburgh Woollen Mill.

Three Light Sign

There is a certain railway line
that runs straight through your town.
The level crossing's three light sign,
a therefore upside down,

has never blocked my route to you.
Perhaps my speed alarms
its sense of pace. When I drive through
the crossing's up in arms

but it has never told me stop
so I have never learned.
Attempts at sense have been a flop,
a therefore overturned.

You're always either in your room
or wandering about
outside. The crossing, I assume,
knows not to let you out.

I like to think it's in control
in case I go too far.
How underrated, on the whole,
most level crossings are.

You've given me a few bad nights –
ranting, withdrawn or worse
but when I see the crossing lights,
a therefore in reverse,

I know you don't mean any harm.
That's just the way it goes.
You, like the level crossing arm,
must have your highs and lows.

Sometimes two things that shouldn't mix
cannot be kept apart.
There is a rift too deep to fix
between a stop, a start,

a car, a train. But I see ways
over contested land,
watching the level crossing raise
its firm, permissive hand.

Driving Me Away

I caught the train to Waterloo,
The tube to Leicester Square.
Both did what they set out to do,
But neither could compare
With your closed eyes, your bitten nails
And the oddness you display.
You beat whatever's on the rails
At driving me away.

The coach to Gatwick last July
Did it in record time.
The plane, once it had deigned to fly,
Managed an upward climb.
You beat whatever's in the air
Or on the motorway
And do not even charge a fare
For driving me away.

The transit van I hired to move
For which I had to pack
Box after box, as if to prove
I wasn't coming back
And before driving which I paid
A visit to the tip,
Just to ensure the point was made:
This was a one way trip –

You beat that too. I could name loads
Of engine-powered things
In oceans, in the clouds, on roads,
With carriages or wings
But you could nudge them all off track
With the mad things you say.
No car could ever have your knack
Of driving me away.

There's not a lot that you can do
Well, or indeed at all.
I must appreciate your few
Talents. When taxis stall
Or when friends offer me a lift
And there's a slight delay
I am reminded of your gift
For driving me away.

Paint a Closed Window

We stood side by side.
Only George walked on.
You spoke and I replied
        but I had gone.

My gone did not depend
on anything you'd planned
and I did not extend
        even a hand.

My gone was not the sort
that might come back one day.
It was less felt than thought
        but most away.

I looked the same to you,
the arches and the cars,
and you could not see through
        my skin to bars.

My arrow pointed north.
Your word had lost its pass,
so no more back and forth
        from the hourglass.

My face became a chart
where pleasantries were drawn.
The binman pulled his cart
        around the lawn

where we stood once removed,
where we stand twice returned.
Nothing can be improved
        my gone has learned.

Foolish to have supposed
there might be other ways.
Paint a closed window, closed
        is how it stays.

I am prepared to face
how fleeting I have been
to you and to this place,
        that tree, the green

circle of grass, the stone.
From your first fixed-term kiss
I knew I could not own
        any of this.

Minus Fingers

What craftsmen sometimes do to glass
Or children to balloons,
You do (or did, since presents pass –
Shade of infrequent moons),

What lovers, as the distance grows,
Do with a hand and kiss.
Some do to bubbles or a nose
What you have done to this.

What stylists, after wash and cut,
Do to their clients' hair.
What the wind does to make doors shut
Using no more than air.

How brass band players get the sound
Out of their golden horns,
How breezes move one leaf around
Several connecting lawns,

Is how you've treated what you had,
Like football referees
To whistles when a move is bad
Enough for penalties.

You've done what someone does who spends
Money they can't afford.
So let's compare you with said friends
And see how well you've scored.

Your nose is still a chain of blocks.
Your power on the pitch
Is non-existent, Liquid-locks-
For-hair. You weren't once rich

So you enjoyed no spending spree.
You have no crystal zoo.
You can scare no one noisily
Piercing the things you blew.

You've got no notes to make a tune,
No fragile fluid spheres
To demonstrate how fast, how soon
Everything disappears,

No kiss that soars above flat land.
I count what can be shown,
In minus fingers on my hand,
For everything you've blown.

Never Away from You

(commissioned by Friends of the Earth/Poems on the Buses 1998, to go on a London bus)

Start at King's Cross and head for Waterloo.
People should read this verse from East to West,
Always towards, never away from you.

I need some kind bus drivers, just a few
To take my lines the way that I suggest:
Start at King's Cross and head for Waterloo.

Passengers at the bus stop in a queue
Must change their routes and see that mine's the best:
Always towards, never away from you.

Alternative directions will not do.
All other destinations fail my test.
Start at King's Cross and head for Waterloo.

If London Transport bosses only knew
What was at stake, they'd see my words progressed
Always towards, never away from you.

They'd help this poem get from CB2
To RG40, properly addressed,
Start at King's Cross and head for Waterloo,
Always towards, never away from you.

Men to Burn

The same man every year;
though we have men to burn
we have sealed off that idea.
It is still one man's turn.

Every year one man glows,
his bright flesh chars to dim
and every next year shows
we are not rid of him.

He is propped against a fence.
His embroidered teeth still flash.
I part with twenty pence
to convert him into ash

but he won't stay ash for long.
He reappears in rags,
features not quite so strong
and his legs in dustbin bags.

He will keep coming back
for as long as he is allowed.
He will turn from gold to black
if he knows he's got a crowd.

I should have said this before
but I'm not prepared to pay
to bring him back once more
or to make him go away.

I don't like his grey sock face
or this year's cushion knees.
A good man in the first place
makes for better effigies.

The Norbert Dentressangle Van

I heave my morning like a sack
of signs that don't appear,
say August, August, takes me back…
      That it was not this year…
say greenness, greenness, that's the link…
      That they were different trees
does not occur to those who think
in anniversaries.

I drive my morning like a truck
with a backsliding load,
say bastard, bastard, always stuck
      behind him on the road
(although I saw another man
      in a distinct machine
last time a Dentressangle van
was on the A14).

I draw my evening like a blind,
say darkness, darkness, that's
if not the very then the kind…
      That I see only slats…
say moonlight, moonlight, shines the same…
      That it's a streetlamp's glow
might be enough to take the name
from everything we know.

I sketch my evening like a plan.
I think I recognise
the Norbert Dentressangle van…
      That mine are clouded eyes…
say whiteness, whiteness, that's the shade…
      That paint is tins apart
might mean some progress can be made
in worlds outside the heart.

First of the Last Chances

Long for This World

I settle for less than snow,
try to go gracefully as seasons go

which will regain their ground –
ditch, hill and field – when a new year comes round.

Now I know everything:
how winter leaves without resenting spring,

lives in a safe time frame,
gives up so much but knows he can reclaim

all titles that are his,
fall out for months and still be what he is.

I settle for less than snow:
high only once, then no way up from low,

then to be swept from drives.
Ten words I throw into your changing lives

fly like ten snowballs hurled:
I hope to be, and will, long for this world.

You Won't Find a Bath in Leeds

From the River Cam and the A14
To the Aire and the tall M1,
We left the place where home had been,
Still wondering what we'd done,
And we went to Yorkshire, undeterred
By the hearts we'd left down south
And we couldn't believe the words we heard
From the lettings agent's mouth.

He showed us a flat near an abbatoir,
Then one where a man had died,
Then one with nowhere to park our car
Then one with no bath inside.
With the undertone of cheering
Of a person who impedes,
He looked straight at us, sneering,
'You won't find a bath in Leeds.'

'We have come to Leeds from Cambridge.
We have heard that Leeds is nice.
A bath is seen in Cambridge
As an integral device,
So don't tell me that a shower
Is sufficient to meet my needs,'
I said. I received a glower
And, 'You won't find a bath in Leeds.'

He fingered a fraying curtain
And I said, 'You can't be sure.
Some things in life are uncertain
And that's what hope is for.
One day I might meet Robert Redford
At Bristol Temple Meads.
I've found baths in Bracknell and Bedford
And I might find a bath in Leeds.'

He replied with a refutation
Which served to increase our pain
But we didn't head for the station
Or run for a rescue train,
Though we felt like trampled flowers
Who'd been set upon by weeds.
We told him to stuff his showers
And we would find a bath in Leeds.

Some people are snide and scathing
And they try to undermine
Your favourite form of bathing
Or the way you write a line.
At night, while you're busy praying
That your every plan succeeds,
There are killjoys somewhere saying,
'You won't find a bath in Leeds.'

A better definition
Might be reading all of Proust,
But the concept of ambition
Has been radically reduced.
While the London wits are burning
Their cash in the Groucho Club,
In Yorkshire we're simply yearning
To locate an enamel tub.

I win, Mr Bath Bad Tiding.
I have not one bath but two.
En-suite in the sweet West Riding
And no bloody thanks to you.
I may never run fast, or tower
Over Wimbledon's top seeds
Or hit sixes like David Gower
But I have found a bath in Leeds.

Out of This World

Cannot remember grass between my toes
or how it feels when feet and tarmac touch.
Cannot recall my life before I rose
and I have had to rise above so much

that first I hit the roof-rack of the car,
then my ascent bent back a lamp post's head.
I have, without exception and so far,
risen above a tower of what's been said,

above a mountain range of what's been done
to people, books and cities that I love.
I'll risk head-on collision with the sun
if I have one more thing to rise above.

What if the risen suffocate in space?
You send us up, not knowing where we'll go.
Would it be such a terrible disgrace
if just this once, I were to sink below

the quilted warmth of your intended slur,
your next offence, soft as a feather bed?
I'd prove more difficult to disinter
than knobbly tree roots or the tenured dead

and after having done my stint in blue
and subsequent to equal time in green
it will not matter if I dropped or flew
out of this world. Out of this world, I mean.

Wells-Next-the-Sea

I came this little seaside town
And went a pub they call The Crown
Where straight away I happened see
A man who seemed quite partial me.
I proved susceptible his charms
And fell right in his open arms.
From time time, every now and then,
I hope meet up with him again.

Six of One

I put it to my indecisive friend:
we step up our surveillance of the shops.
He shakes his head and says he'd like to spend
some time in jail, one year or two years, tops,
to ascertain which he prefers, the robbers or the cops.

He sighs and mentions double-sided coins.
He knows full well that his reaction peeves
his colleagues, but he argues if he joins
a bad crowd for a while, then when he leaves
he'll know for sure he likes policemen slightly more than thieves.

I say he couldn't stand two years inside.
True, he replies, *but think of my release.*
I can't confirm what's right until I've tried
what's wrong. He tells me I'm the one he'll fleece.
I grin. He might like confrontation rather more than peace.

Gently, I tell him not to be a fool.
Why not? he says. He tried the bottom set
before the top at comprehensive school.
I say *Remember…* No. He might forget.
He's not convinced that credit suits him any more than debt.

Listen, I shout, *that noise.* He bites his nails
while I pursue the yelp of an alarm
to a smashed window. As our siren wails
I grab my indecisive partner's arm
hoping by now he feels protection has the edge on harm.

He shrugs me off. No progress has been made
since his long, non-committal day began.
I scream *It's over! Finished!* – a tirade
that would provoke a more conclusive man.
He asks me why I think this sort of ending's better than

Seasonal Dilemma

Another Christmas compromise. Let's drink another toast.
Once more we failed to dodge the things that put us out the most.
To solve this timeless riddle I would crawl from coast to coast:
Which is worse at Christmas, to visit or to host?

To spend a week with relatives and listen to them boast,
Try not to look too outraged when they make you eat nut roast
Or have them drive their pram wheels over each new morning's post?
Which is worse at Christmas, to visit or to host?

Dickens, you let me down. You should have made Scrooge ask
the ghost
Which is worse at Christmas, to visit or to host?

Second-hand Advice for a Friend

I used to do workshops in schools quite a lot
And some classes were good, although others were not,
And when sessions went wrong, in no matter what way,
There was one standard phrase every teacher would say.

Each time couplets were questioned by gum-chewing thugs
In reluctant time out from the dealing of drugs,
Some poor teacher would utter the desperate plea:
'Show Sophie Hannah how good you can be.'

This phenomenon cannot be simply explained
Since I don't think it's something they learned when they trained.
You do not have to say, for your PGCE,
'Show Sophie Hannah how good you can be.'

You do not have to say it to work or to live
But compared with advice that I've heard teachers give
Such as, 'Don't eat in classrooms' or 'Straighten your tie',
I've arrived at the view that it ranks pretty high.

Outside the school gates, in the world of grown men,
It's a phrase I'm inclined to recite now and then.
I don't see why I shouldn't extend its remit
On the offchance it might be a nationwide hit.

I've a friend who I reckon could use it. And how.
We've had a nice day so let's not spoil it now.
I am no kind of teacher, and yet I can see
That you're not in the place where you clearly should be.

No answering back – just return to the fold.
We'll have none of your cheek and you'll do as you're told
By the staff of Leeds Grammar, St Mark's and Garth Hill,
All those manifestations of teacherly will

Who join dozens of voices in dozens of schools
That make grownups of children and wise men of fools.
Stop behaving like someone who's out of his tree.
Show Sophie Hannah how good you can be.

Dark Mechanic Mills

A car is a machine. It's not organic.
It is a man-made thing that can be fixed,
Maybe by you, as you are a mechanic
Although I must admit that I have mixed
Feelings about your skills in this connection.
You shrug and say my engine sounds 'right rough'.
Shouldn't you, then, proceed with an inspection?
Looking like Magnus Mills is not enough.

Resemblance to a Booker Prize contender
Has a quaint charm but only goes so far.
When servicing formed the entire agenda,
When I had no real trouble with my car,
Our whole relationship was based upon it,
This likeness, but you can't go in a huff
If I suggest you open up the bonnet.
Looking like Magnus Mills is not enough.

I lay all my suggestions on the table:
Fuel pump or filter, alternator, clutch,
The coil or the accelerator cable
Or just plain yearning for the oily touch
Of a soft rag in a mechanic's fingers.
That's not your style at all. You merely grin.
Is it your Booker confidence that lingers?
I don't know why. You didn't even win.

You laugh as if you can't see what the fuss is
When I explain my car keeps cutting out.
I know that Magnus Mills has driven buses;
That's not the way I choose to get about.
I'm sorry that it has to end so badly
But I am up to here with being towed
And I'd take a clone of Jeffrey Archer, gladly,
If he could make my car move down the road.

Martins Heron Heart

No doctor cares enough
to analyse the content of my veins,
my blood that bears a rough
resemblance to a Stagecoach South West Trains
timetable. Start, please start,
Wokingham Bracknell Martins Heron heart.

Send a mechanic, quick,
the best you have. Should your mechanic fail
to get me going, stick
me on a train to Egham, Sunningdale,
Virginia Water, Staines.
It's true; those Waterloo to Reading trains

prove all your theories wrong –
medicine, science. I am on the mend,
doctor, thanks to a long
list of the Sunday running times. Attend
my bedside. Tick your chart.
Wokingham   Bracknell   Martins Heron   heart

Tide to Land

I know the rules and hear myself agree
Not to invest beyond this one night stand.
I know your pattern: in, out, like the sea.
The sharp north wind must blow away the sand.

Soon my supply will meet your last demand
And you will have no further use for me.
I will not swim against the tide to land.
I know the rules and hear myself agree.

I've kept a stash of hours, just two or three
To smuggle off your coast like contraband.
We will both manage (you more easily)
Not to invest beyond this one night stand.

To narrow-minded friends I will expand
On cheap not being the same as duty-free.
I'll say this was exactly what I planned.
I know your pattern: in, out, like the sea.

It's not as if we were designed to be
Strolling along the beach front, hand in hand.
Things change, of natural necessity.
The sharp north wind must blow away the sand

And every storm to rage, however grand,
Will end in pain and shipwreck and debris
And each time there's a voice I have to strand
On a bare rock, hardened against its plea.
I know the rules.

The Shadow Tree

In the lake, a reflected tree dangles
while its counterpart squats on the land.
Together they look, from some angles,
like a hand growing out of a hand.
Trunk to trunk, bark to water, they stand.

One is real, that would be the contention,
while the other, illusion or fake,
is a trick of the light, an invention
of the skin on the top of the lake.
I am here for the shadow tree's sake,

for its unannounced coming and going
(no one plants, no one chops). I would give
anything for a shadow tree, knowing,
as its branches get caught in the sieve
of the surface of water and live

for a glance of the moon, moments only,
that the dark fabrication I saw
was a miracle, not like the lonely
unexceptional lump on the shore,
such a stickler for natural law

with its sap, its botanical listing
and its representation at Kew,
its pedantic disciples, insisting
that one cannot be both false and true.
We are shadow trees. That's what we do.

He is Now a Country Member

He is now a country member.
The subscription rate goes down.
January to December,
If you live or work in town

You pay more. You come more often
And the fee, therefore, is high.
In a vain attempt to soften
Last year's blow, he now drops by.

Not a word since last September.
He left town. We both know why.
He says, 'I'm a country member.'
'I remember,' I reply.

Silk Librarian

We have a silk librarian,
One who behaves and looks
Just like a real librarian
When lending people books.
We lost our first librarian
Then others of her ilk.
We need a good librarian
And so we've gone for silk.

A silk librarian endures.
The paid and unpaid bills
Are neatly filed in metal drawers.
Eye-drops, inhalers, pills –
Gone. We no longer house the cures
For the imagined ills
Of real librarians with flaws
That far outweigh their skills.

Real flowers used to be displayed.
They died and made a mess.
Genuine salaries were paid.
Silk wages cost us less,
Though, over time, the colours fade
From eyes and hair and dress.
Every two years or so, upgrade
To maximise success.

Feel free to disapprove, protest
At what you never knew
Until just now, and never guessed
And cannot prove untrue.
A sin too many, once confessed,
Becomes a sin too few.
While you deny that silk is best
We cut the silk for you.

God's Eleventh Rule

I want to sit beside the pool all day,
Swim now and then, read *Peeping Tom*, a novel
By Howard Jacobson. You needn't pay
To hire a car to drive me to a hovel
Full of charred native art. Please can I stay
Behind? I will if necessary grovel.
I want to sit beside the pool all day,
Swim now and then, read *Peeping Tom*, a novel.

Pardon? You're worried I will find it boring?
My days will be repetitive and flat?
You think it would be oodles more alluring
To see the chair where Mao Tse Tung once sat.
Novels and pools are all I need for touring,
My *Peeping Tom*, *Nostromo* after that.
Pardon? You're worried I will find it boring?
My days will be repetitive and flat.

Okay, so you were right about *Nostromo*,
But I've a right to stay in this hotel.
Sienna: I refused to see *il duomo*.
(Does that mean Mussolini? Who can tell?)
In Spain I told them, 'Baño, bebo, como.'
I shunned the site where Moorish warriors fell.
Okay, so you were right about *Nostromo*
But I've a right to stay in this hotel.

I'm so alarmed, my voice becomes falsetto
When you prescribe a trip round local slums.
Would I drag you from Harvey Nicks to Netto?
No I would not. Down, down go both my thumbs.
I'm happy in this five-star rich man's ghetto
Where teeth are, by and large, attached to gums.
I'm so alarmed, my voice becomes falsetto
When you prescribe a trip round local slums.

It's not an English thing. No need to grapple
With the strange ways we foreigners behave.
My colleague would be thrilled to see your chapel,
Turrets and frescos and your deepest cave,
But as for me, I'd rather watch sun dapple
The contours of a chlorinated wave.
It's not an English thing. No need to grapple
With the strange ways we foreigners behave.

I want to spend all day beside the pool.
I wish that this were needless repetition,
But next to you, a steroid-guzzling mule,
A hunger strike and the first Christian mission
Look apathetic. God's eleventh rule:
Thou shalt get sore feet at an exhibition.
I want to spend all day beside the pool.
I wish that this were needless repetition.

Where to Look

The leaves that this year brought
next year won't bring again.
If autumn has one thought
it is not *where?* but *when?*

Summer is on the ground
long before winter's sting.
The loss must be profound
to make us hunt for spring.

Eyes down, we find it dead,
red powder at our feet
but staring straight ahead
we see its green wings beat,

all future and no past,
baffled as winter grieves.
Next year, not this or last,
is where to look for leaves.

Brief Encounter

I loved you and I left you at the station.
I watched you on the platform and I waved,
Taking in every scrap of information.
Every last detail of your face, I saved,

Thinking that when the engine started running
And as the train proceeded down the track,
You'd shrink, then disappear. But love is cunning:
The station café faded into black,

So did the world around you and beside you.
You alone seemed to grow. In broken hearts
Both distance and perspective are denied you.
Love looks no smaller as the train departs.

The Cycle

I cannot stay – I'm not the one deserting –
Or go; you are no longer here to leave.
I can't forgive, not without also hurting,
Forget, or I'll be even more naïve.
I can't confer; I'd feel that I was cheating.
I can't concede a case I've never fought
Or win and not administer a beating.
I cannot settle in or out of court,
Can't give in case I implicate the taker,
Can't take from everyone with ground to give
And gather acre on untended acre
When I need just a few square feet to live,
Can't end this in a neat or messy way.
I cannot start again. I cannot stay.

Black River

I asked to return to my original love
but I gave the wrong code and access was denied.
The clocks go back, though by no means far enough.
My white form came up green on the other side.
        It was so long since I had tried
that to do so was both a relief and a source of pride.

I asked to return to my original niche.
My house and furniture at Black River, I wrote,
then read it through. It read like a limp pastiche.
My white form came out smeared as a ransom note.
        I decided I must devote
more time to the box marked *Enter witty anecdote*.

I asked to return to my original ground.
Original, scoffed the clerk, *like there's such a thing.*
I thought his procedures all the more unsound
for being based on a rusty playground swing.
        Above us, a blackbird's wing
made a powerful case for never really bothering.

I asked to return to my original point,
but was that a person, a place or a state of mind?
A man in the queue shouted out *Let's split this joint*
so I shared my stash and he left it all behind
        singing *We, the undersigned,*
don't know. Then I wandered off, and what should I find?

Well, what I should find (though I cannot say that I did
since the arrows were keen to point towards something new
and all known rows, whether Savile, Death or Skid
had become the past, the ephemera and the view)
        is that none of it is true.
Go back to the starting line. Your original love is you.

The Cancellation

On the day of the cancellation
The librarian phoned at two.
My reading at Swillingcote Youth Club
Had regrettably fallen through.

The members of Swillingcote Youth Club
Had just done their GCSEs
And demanded a rave, not poems,
Before they began their degrees.

Since this happened at such short notice
They would still have to pay my fee.
I parked in the nearest lay-by
And let out a loud yippee.

The librarian put the phone down
And muttered, 'Oh, thank the Lord!'
She was fed up of chaperoning
While the touring poet toured.

The girl from the local bookshop
Who'd been told to provide a stall
But who knew that the youth club members
Would buy no books at all

Expressed with a wild gyration
Her joy at a late reprieve,
And Andy, the youth club leader,
And the youth arts worker, Steve,

Both cheered as one does when granted
The gift of eternal life.
Each felt like God's chosen person
As he skipped back home to his wife.

It occurred to me some time later
That such bliss, such immense content,
Needn't always be left to fortune,
Could in fact be a planned event.

What ballet or play or reading,
What movie creates a buzz
Or boosts the morale of the nation
As a cancellation does?

No play, is the simple answer.
No film that was ever shown.
I submit that the cancellation
Is an art form all of its own.

To give back to a frantic public
Some hours they were sure they'd lose
Might well be my new vocation.
I anticipate great reviews.

From now on, with verve and gusto
I'll agree to a month-long tour.
Call now if you'd like to book me
For three hundred pounds or more.

The Guest Speaker

I have to keep myself awake
While the guest speaker speaks.
For his and for procedure's sake
I have to keep myself awake.
However long his talk might take
(And, Christ, it feels like weeks)
I have to keep myself awake
While the guest speaker speaks.

Everyone in the Changing Room

11 September 2001

Everyone in the changing room pronounced it a disgrace.
He'll get short shrift in Baildon if he dares to show his face.
He needs a damn good seeing to, that's what all his lot need,
    Everyone in the changing room agreed.

Everyone in the changing room reckons he's lying low.
The hot ones from the sauna want to tell him where to go.
The cold ones from the plunge pool say someone should start a fund.
    Everyone in the changing room is stunned.

Everyone in the changing room is certain it was him,
Young mothers from aerobics and the runners from the gym
And when they said it's mental, this, and there's no end in sight,
    Everyone in the changing room was right.

Everyone in the changing room would fight for this good cause.
We swim our lengths and lift our weights; you'll want us in your wars.
There will be no more tragedies, no waste or pain or loss
    When everyone in the changing room is boss.

Away-day

Dear baby the size of an olive,
Advise me on how to proceed.
On Thursday we've got an away-day
Which will be very boring indeed.

We'll be trapped in a room with no windows,
Doing things of no value at all
And I shudder to think how much nonsense
Will drift through the uterine wall.

You might hear the name David Blunkett.
Forget it as soon as you can
And look forward to treats that are pending
Like your first ever ultrasound scan.

Dear baby the size of an olive
I can't take you away from all this
But in seven months no one can touch us.
Think of all the grim meetings we'll miss:

All those votes for more rules and less freedom.
What a fine time I picked to conceive.
Down with what is now called education
And hurrah for maternity leave.

Mother-to-be

*Eating a good balanced diet, taking plenty of exercise and fresh air and
finding the time to relax when you're away from work will improve your
chances of conceiving a healthy baby... You should take particular care to
cut down on 'social drugs'. Cannabis is known to interfere with the normal
production of sperm. It is also thought that LSD can cause birth defects.*

(from New Pregnancy and Birth Book *by Dr Miriam Stoppard*)

Ideally your floors should not be carpeted but tiled.
A brightly coloured nursery will stimulate your child.
Do not eat soft-boiled eggs, smoke crack, fellate infected men
But tell your partner how you feel (see diagram, page ten).

You're bored and restless? Now is not the time to fly to China
Or to let friends with litter trays blow air up your vagina.
Make sure your fitness trainer is aware of your condition.
Remember, you must check your teeth and call that electrician

And every time you raise a glass or lift a fork, please think
Is this the very best thing for your child to eat or drink?
Once-a-month treats – a slice of cake – will not do any harm
But don't lick lambing ewes or stick syringes in your arm.

Quite often pregnancies go wrong, and when they do, that's sad.
It sometimes happens if you're stressed or pregnant by your dad
But eat your folic acid and next time a thin blue line
Appears, relax. Think positive. Most likely you'll be fine.

Try not to feel too daunted by this barrage of advice.
It really doesn't matter if you slip up once or twice –
Eat the wrong cheese, go on the game. It's not all doom and gloom:
Never again will baby be as safe as in your womb.

Now and Then

'Now that I'm fifty-seven,'
My mother used to say,
'Why should I waste a minute?
Why should I waste a day

Doing the things I ought to
Simply because I should?
Now that I'm fifty-seven
I'm done with that for good.'

But now and then I'd catch her
Trapped in some thankless chore
Just as she might have been at
Fifty-three or fifty-four

And I would want to say to her
(And have to bite my tongue)
That if you mean to learn a skill
It's well worth starting young

And so, to make sure I'm in time
For fifty, I've begun
To do exactly as I please
Now that I'm thirty-one.

Healing Powers

My foot is blue and bloated.
The swelling won't go down.
My limp is duly noted
As I hobble through the town.
I pass a Reiki master.
Of course! I should have put
The two together faster:
Healing powers, my foot.

I take my sore size seven
And place it in his hands.
It's ten now. By eleven
I'll be sprinting to the sands.
I ponder such remission.
My tears, like magic, dry.
Pure chance or superstition?
Healing powers, my eye.

My walking looks much better –
I jump, I jog, I hike,
Reluctant to upset a
Reiki master whom I like
But the pain is most dismaying
And I must confess, I put
New conviction in the saying:
Healing powers, my foot.

Homeopathy

She told me negativity was bad.
I said it wasn't, not the kind I had.

She told me that the people I resent
will have their own accounts of each event.

She said it wasn't up to me to judge
and that I should examine every grudge

and ask myself if those I cannot stand
are those who hold a mirror in each hand

reflecting back to me the awful fact
of who I am, unwelcome and exact.

She said there was no need to feel a threat.
I said suspicion was my safety net.

I'd allow harmless men misunderstood
if she'd allow the opposite of good.

Of course, she said, malevolence exists.
Respond with anger, though, and it persists

whereas apply benevolence like balm
and often you can soothe the rash of harm.

I did not feel my interests would be served
by spreading peace where it was not deserved.

What about standards, justice, right and wrong?
She said our meeting had gone on too long

and that the remedy that she'd prescribed
right from the start, if properly imbibed,

erodes those thoughts that play a harmful role
leaving what's beneficial to the whole

person (in this case, me). If this is true
then since I did just what she told me to –

taking my medicine, the right amount
at the right time – surely she can't discount

the feelings that remain. She should concede
that these must be exactly what I need

and that my grudge, impassive and immense,
is good for me, in a holistic sense.

I proved my point like a triumphant kid.
She laughed a lot. I gave her sixty quid.

Your Turn Next

You don't know where he's been.
You only saw him in a magazine,
        don't know what kind of life he's had,
    whether he's manic, violent, a fad.

    You don't know where he went
after the club, the sort of things he spent
        his pocket money on, the bit
    of trouble he was in. You don't know shit.

    He is a scrap of text
to you. He is the words *it's your turn next*,
        deal of the week, the longed-for link
    between you and the thoughts you failed to think.

    You don't know what he means –
philanthropy or company or genes.
            Can he play tennis? How's his serve?
    Are you what he will grow up to deserve?

    Seventeen years from now,
after too many lagers and a row,
            I'll turn up. Yes in your backyard.
    It's your turn next, so take it. Take it hard.

You misconstrue his tone.
You cannot seem to reach him on the phone.
He swore those plants were watercress.
He is a stranger and you want him less,

a psycho boy. A lout.
You don't remember, as you throw me out,
that, give or take a wait and see,
I'm only saying what you said to me.

To a Certain Person

If one day I should find myself in pain,
In a predicament or in distress,
There's something you can do for me: refrain
From digging out my number and address.

Don't send your sympathy or kind regards.
Don't send your cash (as if you ever would),
Nor are your presents, telegrams and cards
Evidence that you wish me all things good.

You will profess to want to help. Then do –
A burst of honesty might make me smile.
Tell me that you believe I'm overdue
This, if not even more severe a trial.

Indulge yourself: applaud, rejoice, enthuse
And maybe soon I'll have some more bad news.

0208

Instead of telephoning every place
that is connected in your mind to me
and then concluding I am hard to trace
when Jill at my recruitment agency,
despite your cloth shoes and your honest face
and all the charm with which you plead your case,
explains the rule (quite proper, you agree)
of client confidentiality,

why not pursue some of those little scraps
of paper where my number's scrawled in pen?
They can't have travelled far, unless perhaps
you've been to the North Pole and back again.
Look in the pockets of your shirts, the gaps
between your piles of books, shake out the maps
stuffed in your glove compartment. Businessmen
ask for a card; you've taken nine or ten.

In many botched attempts to be discreet,
you hide my number where it can't be found
even by you, which strikes me more as sweet
than irritating. On the underground,
at King's Cross, Ealing Broadway, Warren Street,
commuters shake it daily from their feet.
The way you must have scattered it around
defeats your object. One day it is bound

to fall unbidden from a jacket sleeve
not at a moment you or I would choose.
Lies will be called for, harder to believe
when the same number tumbles from your shoes.
This doesn't worry you. You're so naïve,
but all I know is, each time you retrieve
the number you perpetually lose
it is a minor triumph, front page news.

You tell me I'm elusive, and your tone
Is that of hunter after catching prey,
sort of *Aha, I've got you on the phone,*
I've tracked you down, you'll never get away.
Thank you for the initiative you've shown.
Long may your absent-mindedness postpone
and your continued scattiness delay
the wind that carries novelties away.

Leave

Look at the street lights in the square
That should project an orange sky,
Then note the darkness everywhere.
They do not work, and nor do I.

This television, lost at sea,
Emits an endless, wordless roar.
It needs to be replaced. Like me,
It is not working any more.

The sunken car beside the road
Whose hazards blink that extra mile
Wants nothing more than to be towed.
It won't be working for a while.

Neither will I. You mustn't mind
Or take offence if I suggest
You learn the art of being kind
To everything that needs a rest.

Notice the fifteen forty-nine
Never quite makes it out of sight.
There is a problem with the line
So it returns. I also might.

Ante-Natal

My husband doesn't want to hold the plastic pelvis model.
He tells the other husbands that it's bound to be a doddle.
He thinks the role of classes is to teach, not mollycoddle.
      He'll go so far, but not an inch beyond.

My husband is afraid of meeting women called Magenta,
Of sharing wholesome snacks outside the Early Learning Centre,
Of any exercise that's an incontinence preventor.
      He's friendly but determined not to bond.

My husband listens to my fear, tells me to overcome it,
Changes the subject to the Davos Economic Summit,
Decides that if there's pain he'll simply ask the nurse to numb it.
      He says he doesn't think it sounds that bad.

My husband mocks the books with their advice about nutrition,
He shocks the other couples in the coffee intermission
By saying Ziggy Marley seems in pretty good condition
      Despite the smoking habits of his dad.

My husband doesn't care if I'm a leaner or a squatter,
Says pregnancy is no excuse for reading *Harry Potter*.
He isn't keen on Stephanie or Amos or Carlotta.
      Leave it to him; he named our latest car.

On Father's Day my husband gets a card he's not expecting.
I say it's from the baby, with a little redirecting.
He doesn't blame my hormones or insist that I'm projecting.
      He tells me he's the father of a star.

On Westminster Bridge

I don't believe the building of a bridge
Should be an image that belongs to peace.
Raised eyebrow or the river's hardened ridge,
It wouldn't want hostilities to cease.
Aloof, on tiptoes, it deserts each side
For the high ground and, though it has to touch
Land that real lives have made undignified,
I don't believe it likes that very much.
It knows that every time we try to cross
To a new place, old grudges bind our feet.
It holds out little hope and feels no loss,
Indifferent more than neutral, when we meet
Halfway to transfer ownership of blame,
Then both of us go back the way we came.

Ballade of the Rift

Two enemies at once I lost.
It was a heavy price to pay.
I thought that I could bear the cost
Of an impromptu mercy day.
Now I'm invited out to play
And find I feel distinctly miffed
With no fracas, no feud, no fray;
I yearn to instigate a rift.

Wildly and wantonly I tossed
My horde of grievances away.
Above my inner ice and frost
I forged the sun's most radiant ray,
Now, with its heaps of UVA,
Summer's a burden, not a gift.
I miss the grime, the grot, the grey.
I yearn to instigate a rift.

I rue the day I blithely glossed
Over my foes' misdeeds, while they
Try not to boss where once they bossed,
Promise to honour and obey.
To look for peers among one's prey
Requires too great a mental shift,
And as they wheedle, cringe and bray
I yearn to instigate a rift.

Preachers and shrinks and healers say
Forgiveness gives the heart a lift –
Good on them. Be that as it may
I yearn to instigate a rift.

Wedding Poem

for Rachel and Ian

Marriage's rather grand accommodation
Can make a budding love succeed or fail.
We stumble in and ask for information
Regarding all the properties for sale
And marriage is the price-on-application
Castle with grounds, moat, lake and nature trail.

Some kid themselves and think they can afford it
And when their love runs out it's repossessed
While others, who do better in love's audit
And whose allegiances deserve the best
Because they are the best, those ones can lord it
Over the squabbling and half-hearted rest.

Today the castle has its rightful buyer,
Its asking price, and it will not be trumped
Because the bidding can't go any higher;
This is a love that will not be gazumped
By any other applicant, hard-trier
Or any living heart that ever thumped.

Marriage is love's new house. Love has invested
Its savings wisely, bought the place outright.
It has had several flats, and it has rested
Its head in many a hotel and campsite.
This is the best of all the homes it's tested.
This is where it will sleep now, every night.

Royal Wedding Poem

*This poem was commissioned by the Daily Mail, to commemorate the
marriage of Prince Edward and Sophie Rees-Jones. It was never printed.*

I have attended weddings in the past
Where I'm the only person in the room
To harbour an intransigent and vast
Landmass of spite towards the bride and groom.
I have attended weddings with my coat
Buttoned against the hot, ecstatic horde
Throughout the service, wearing a remote
Glaze to appear above it all and bored.

At last, a marriage I can celebrate:
No choruses of 'Oh, you have to come!',
No one I liked once but have grown to hate
But must make small-talk with to please my mum.
Weddings involving nobody one knows –
What a good plan. I'll vote for more of those.

GODISNOWHERE (Now Read Again)

Sign outside a Bradford church

1.　Go, Di. Snow here.

(as read by a woman called Diane who is contemplating booking a holiday somewhere hot)

2.　Go dis now her E.

(as read by a concerned father who is hoping to persuade his teenage daughter to stop taking drugs by appealing to her in a more contemporary dialect)

3.　God is now? Here? Now? Read again.

(as read by a philosopher who, on finding himself unable to settle the question of whether the concept of an almighty is a temporal or a spatial one, decides he needs to do more research)

4.　God is nowhere. Now read again.

(There is no supreme being. You might as well settle for a good book.)

Metaphysical Villanelle

'We may or may not cease to exist' – conclusion of a long, late-night discussion about religion on an Arvon course at Lumb Bank

We have argued for hours and this is the gist.
After much confrontation, at last we agree:
We may or may not cease to exist.

First you scoffed at my view, then in turn I dismissed
Your opinion, but now we've discovered the key.
We have argued for hours and this is the gist:

There is either a god or we're all slightly pissed.
Shall we compromise, since it's now twenty to three?
We may or may not cease to exist.

If I weren't so exhausted I might well insist
That I'm right as a right-thinking person can be
But we've argued for hours and this is the gist:

We can all go to bed without fearing we've missed
Some great spiritual truth. Melvyn's got it, you see –
We may or may not cease to exist.

There isn't a subtext. There isn't a twist
And who cares? Who would like a Ryvita with Brie?
We have argued for hours and this is the gist:
We may or may not cease to exist.

Squirrel's the Word

They're rats with bushy tails, you claim.
They bite and spread disease.
Despite the reassuring name
Of squirrel, they are wild, not tame,
And they belong in trees.

But there's a squirrel that I know
Who calls each day at nine,
Catches the croissant that I throw
And chomps it on the patio.
I think of him as mine.

He is both patient and polite
While I prepare his meal.
Squirrel's the word and it's the right
Word in his case, in fact he's quite
The squirrelish ideal,

So deconstruct him all you please
To bushy tail and rat.
Squirrel is still the name for these
Creatures with squirrels' qualities
And he is just like that.

First of the Last Chances

I stand back as the Skipton train advances,
having to choose too fast

between the scorn and sympathetic glances
of my supporting cast

all of whom think boarding this train enhances
my odds. I wave it past.

If I don't take the first of the last chances
I will not fear the last.

A Woman's Life and Loves

The next eight poems have been set to music by the composer Gabriel Jackson, and form a song cycle that was originally conceived as a contemporary response to the Schumann song cycle Frauenliebe und Leben.

View

I am not lonely. I pretend
that I am here alone.
I do not see your shuttered face
or hear your monotone

but stare instead at roads and fields
and bridges and the sky
and feel the sun's rays on my face.
However hard you try

to substitute your view for mine,
I see the things I see
and am no longer here with you
though you are here with me.

Equals

Each of my false apologies
I retrospectively withdraw.
Yes, there have been discrepancies
Between my conduct and the law.

I have done worse, I have done less
Than promises would have me do,
And as I cheat, as I transgress
I do not give a thought to you.

I sensed that you deserved it then
But took the blame and looked contrite
Before I did the same again,
Thinking the wrong was mine by right

And I enjoyed the risks I took,
The tricks I played, the daily scam.
I have done nothing by the book.
When I professed to give a damn

My smiles, my tears, my words were fake.
Cut me in half; the core was bad
And when you made your big mistake
I can't deny that I was glad

To see, so newly justified
By your descent from fair and true,
The times I lied and lied and lied,
As if I knew. As if I knew.

Postcard

The chances are that by the time you get
This postcard, I'll be home. I will have phoned,
Arranged to meet you and we will have met.
(That day, the day with nothing ruined yet,
No hasty lust or lingering regret,
Decisions and admissions all postponed,
Will be the best we have.) I will have toned
Down what I feel to pleasantries and owned
Up to no thoughts of you beyond the set
Formula: I admire your work. I bet
You will have done the same.
                                    Grateful for this
Chance to stay friends and keep our present lives,
We will arrange another date and miss
Another chance before this card arrives.

Match

Love has not made us good.
We still do all the cynics said we would –
Struggle like heroes searching for a war,
Still want too much, and more.

Love has not made us nice.
Elders and betters with their best advice
Can't stir us from our loungers by the pool.
We dodge all work like school,

Leave urgent debts upaid,
Cancel the solemn promises we've made
If loyalties or circumstances change.
Our thoughts are no less strange,

But love has made us last.
We do together all that in the past
We did alone; err not as one but two
And this is how I knew.

Bridesmaid

A smile or kiss is all you have to spare;
Never a bed, a key, an inch of floor.
All that I am, all that I have, I share,
Yet I possess not half as much but more –
      Double, I swear,
      Though you remain unsure –
Twice what I owned or hoped to own before.

There is no metal weighing down your hand.
You are not subject to the whims of kings
And claim that you will never understand
The pleasure or the point of two gold rings.
      For you no grand
      Passion waits in the wings
Just your own space. A woman needs such things.

Not me, I say. Of all the things to need,
I choose another mind, another face,
Someone of whom, if I were ever freed
I would be tattered remnants or a trace.
      What awkward breed
      Would crave, would even chase
What age and death will bring in any case?

Test

Not easy to relate
This plastic stick, blue line,
To an October date,
A child who might be mine.
Is the blue weak or strong?
How loud the seconds tick
With all that could go wrong.
This blue line, plastic stick
The packet says to use
And then at once discard,
Forgetting that to lose
All that you have is hard
And for a month or so
This plastic stick, blue line
Is all I'll have to show
For what it claims is mine.

Charge

My skin grows taut. What once was soft turns hard
Like silk stretched thinly over sponge or shell.
I count as many bullies in the yard
As any school child desperate for the bell.

Watching my body sprout its suit of arms
Makes me aware of what I must protect,
My charge, who nature won't allow my charms
Alone to guard, much less my intellect.

I fear the notion that I need a shield
But if I run, I'll only rock the cage.
As enemies advance across the field
Cover is no safe substitute for rage.

I am the bearer of a small élite.
I wrap my arms around it in the night
But can't defend a king with my retreat
Whose country is the stomach for a fight.

Favourite

Anyone who prefers the light
Has not explored the dark.
All those who miss the owl in flight
Will lean towards the lark.
She must have heard that Noah halved
The pairs inside the ark
And on its wooden side was carved
The favourite child remark.

I read the message, heard the cheers
And saw the bright award.
I sensed that down the miles and years
A man was overboard,
A man who had been left to drown
And yet remained afloat.
I rinsed the shell dust from my crown.
He swam towards my boat.

The sea is full of souvenirs:
The splinters of the ark,
Bent bottletops and leaking beers,
Noah just one more shark.
I chose the course that I preferred
And will not disembark
I set my compass when I heard
The favourite child remark

So see me now as cabin-hand,
Captain or mutineer,
The scourge or saviour of the land.
I must be both to steer
Free of this sea where, full of ploys,
Old moons resent new suns.
All of my children, girls and boys,
Will be the favourite ones.

Pessimism for Beginners

I

On Her Tiredness

after 'On His Blindness' by John Milton

When I consider how my night is spent,
Either awake or waiting to be woken
From my leased sleep, and never an unbroken
Ten solid hours, I wonder: was I meant
For gigs like this? Somebody should invent
Sleep substitutes, maybe a sleep gift token.
Suddenly it's as if a voice has spoken,
As if this next advice were heaven-sent:
'It's not essential to be sleep-deprived.
Everyone has her limit; you've reached yours.
To struggle on would not be right or fair.
The Lord is quite impressed that you've survived
This long. Invest some cash in a good cause:
They also serve who hire a Swiss au pair.'

Mary Questions the Health Visitor

He never seems to close his eyes.
All night he wants to feed.
If I give in each time he cries,
Will that encourage greed?
How much, exactly, bottles-wise
Does a Messiah need?

I've read *Your Child's Sleep Problems Solved*
And wonder what I've done
To make things worse. Now I've resolved
To cut night feeds to one,
But are more calories involved
In being God's only son?

They say a mother's milk is best.
I'm sure it must be true,
But this one wouldn't take the breast,
Screamed till his face was blue.
Gabriel says it's not a test
And *Cow & Gate* will do

And I should simply smile and nod
At all the smug and trite
Advice I get. My child's not odd;
He's full of love and light,
But how soon will the son of God
Start sleeping through the night?

No doubt you'll think I've got a cheek
For nagging but, dear Lord,
I bore your child – I didn't freak –
Sleep is a fair reward.
And if this lasts another week
I'm phoning Gina Ford.

'No Ball Games etc'

sign outside a London block of flats

Honestly, do we have to spell it out?
No tents, space-hoppers, orgies, Brussels sprout
enthusiasts, no sponsored squirrel fights,
no Ayurvedic quacks, no woolly tights,

no weeping for the joy you think you're owed,
no winking at the house across the road,
dividing rainbows into seven strands
of single colour, no quick show of hands,

no pastry-cutting, origami, chess,
no taking pleasure in your own success,
no sand, no shark impressions, no culottes,
no Christmas pantomimes, no liver spots,

no lurking in the shadows by the shed,
no improvised salutes, no olive bread,
no weightless floating with an auctioneer
in the small pond. No ponds. Hope that's now clear.

Round Robin

Dear Distant Friends,
                          Surprisingly we've still got your addresses,
So here's a list of all our latest triumphs and successes.
This year we've been as busy as a family of beavers
(Though they're just furry animals, while we are high achievers).

We've bought a big new house (my wife corrects me – it's a mansion).
Emily's verses won a prize for prosody and scansion.
Timothy got his partnership and Claire her PhD
Which all reflects extremely well on Dorothy and me.

Our trips abroad (for which we didn't even have to save)
Prove that we're cosmopolitan, cultured and fit and brave:
Kilimanjaro, Venice, San Francisco and Belize.
(Sorry if you can only dream of holidays like these!)

We're thinking of you, humble friends, in terrace/semi/hovel.
We'll be in touch this time next year, but only if you grovel
And say you wish that you were us so much it makes you sick.
Happy New Year to all of you!

Love, Dorothy and Mick

Discipline

after George Herbert's poem of the same name

Throw away thy fag.
Throw away thy match.
    Full-scale drag.
Wear a horrid patch.

Banish heart's desire.
Think of dying young.
    Must aspire
To a cleaner lung.

Not a Marlboro Light
I affect to own,
    But live right,
Work on muscle tone.

Though I fail, I weep,
Neither fit nor slim,
        Yet I creep
To my private gym.

Tony Blair, remove
Ashtrays from the pubs.
        Bars must prove
They are fitness clubs.

Cigarettes are spokes
In the wheel of death.
        (Snog more blokes
If have wholesome breath?)

Nice new healthy law.
Stars of box and screen
        Smoke no more,
Just eat lima bean.

Throw away thy fag.
(Hurry, Blair might catch!)
        How hours drag.
Throw away thy match.

The Plan

Take any mind. Open its doors.
Remove all news, all views on wars,
The thought of censure or applause,

The ratio of slights to cheers.
Peel back the clutter of the years,
Paranoid doubts, ungrounded fears.

Evict the hearsay, then the fact,
The wondering how you should react,
The dream of what your life has lacked,

Smugness for all you have achieved.
Banish whatever you've believed –
All doctrines, proved or preconceived,

All shopping lists, tasks underway,
The papers piled in your in-tray,
Tomorrow, ditto yesterday.

Take your own mind. Knock down the walls.
Let wind gust freely through its halls.
Empty the grand tier, circle, stalls.

Then, with the view completely clear,
Real life as far as it is near,
Sit back and have your best idea.

Letterland

This poem is about language itself.
It uses words in the way it uses words
to demonstrate how those words might be used.
It sends itself up. It is hilarious.
For instance the line 'I am a gibbering fool'.
The line 'Fuckadoodledo'.
It is hilarious.

The first time I read it I hated it, but the second time
I found more in it, more still on the third reading.
I wondered if it might not be about
not finding something easily,
or maybe not, ingeniously not.

I think it's about feeling inadequate
in highly charged emotional situations.
I think it's about time
and how we exist in time,
though when he says 'shuttlecock', of course, he means just that –
shuttlecock.

Fifteen per cent of goodbye...

...doesn't take us much further than g.
It's the edge of a cloud in the sky.
It's the curve of a wave on the sea.
It's the opening bars of the sigh
of a leaf as it falls from the tree.
It's the last thing you'll get from me, that's all –
the last thing you'll get from me.

Deferred Gratification

I am so looking forward to leaving
That I don't want to leave quite yet.
I'll stay put for a few days longer
And delight in how bad things get.

Please neglect me a damn sight harder.
Undermine me and I'll exalt
As I add to my growing collection
Of things which are all your fault.

You've gone back on your word? That's perfect.
Lost your patience with me? Ideal.
My departure, a rolling snowball,
Grows and grows in its cold appeal.

I have lined up a fearless saviour.
I'm rehearsing my freedom dance
So don't stint on your skunk behaviour.
I shall savour it in advance.

I've recorded your every failure
Stretching back to the distant past
But to read you the list of charges
Is a treat that I know can't last,

So I'm saving it up for the weekend,
For my birthday, for Christmas, New Year,
Bonfire Night, Halloween, Thanksgiving.
If there wasn't a loyal, sincere

And intelligent hero waiting
To replace you, I don't suppose
There would be any need to hurry.
I might not leave at all, who knows.

Silly Mummy

What's Mummy doing, Sweetie-Pie?
What's silly Mummy doing?
Let's read a story. No, don't cry.
Look at the cow. She's mooing.

Has Mummy come to spoil our fun?
Does she think you need feeding?
Well, isn't she the silly one?
We don't want milk. We're reading.

Look at the rabbit in his hutch.
Look at the horsey neighing.
Oh yes, we like him very much.
What's silly Mummy saying?

Look at the piggy in his pen.
Oh, isn't Mummy silly?
She's made your milk too hot again.
I know – you like it chilly.

Who's a big fool? Mummy, that's who!
So easy to offend!
Look at the smiley kangaroo
Go bounce, bounce, bounce. The end.

One Little Wish

One little wish slips through the bars,
Flies past the landing strips on stars,
Too light to fall, too high to stand –
A flower launched from a closed hand.

Astronomical

I tell the girl at *Name a Star* of course
I know it's rare, I know she hopes she won't be asked again.
Requests like mine are hardly likely to become the norm.
Most people will continue to conform,

> but I am not most people. I've read the rules. I know what's fair
> and I want to name a star,
> as the blurb says, to show someone I care.

The name I have chosen is David Shithead Stubbs. Now, can we talk
certificates, star lists, gift sets? Oh, go on, let's.

> I've sent my cheque for fifty quid. I have consumer rights.
> She doesn't even ask me what he did.

Do you know how long it took, I say, to choose a slur?
Wanker and arsehole sounded somehow wrong.
Shithead was good but couldn't stand alone,
since how would David Stubbs or anyone have known
the star was named for him? You see, this means
a lot to me. It isn't just a whim.

I need to know that every night, for ever,
he'll trawl the skies, wondering: is that the one?
Feet on the ground, he can repent, appeal, achieve, endeavour
but every twinkle of the star I've named
will show him he is blamed
permanently and hard for what he's done.

> So, David Stubbs, let's see how tough you are.
> I am the customer. I've paid. You can't un-name my star.

The voice I'm speaking to sounds tired. I know
I sound hysterical, a mess,
a shrew it would be foolish to say no to. Well, so be it.
There will be a star called David Shithead Stubbs.
I will lean over balconies to see it.

I give her the address
I want the framed certificate to go to.

Pessimism for Beginners

When you're waiting for someone to e-mail,
When you're waiting for someone to call –
Young or old, gay or straight, male or female –
Don't assume that they're busy, that's all.

Don't conclude that their letter went missing
Or they must be away for a while;
Think instead that they're cursing and hissing –
They've decided you're venal and vile,

That your eyes should be pecked by an eagle.
Oh, to bash in your head with a stone!
But since this is unfairly illegal
They've no choice but to leave you alone.

Be they friend, parent, sibling or lover
Or your most stalwart colleague at work,
Don't pursue them. You'll only discover
That your once-irresistible quirk

Is no longer appealing. Far from it.
Everything that you are and you do
Makes them spatter their basin with vomit.
They loathe Hitler and herpes and you.

Once you take this on board, life gets better.
You give no one your hopes to destroy.
The most cursory phone call or letter
Makes you pickle your heart in pure joy.

It's so different from what you expected!
They do not want to gouge out your eyes!
You feel neither abused nor rejected –
What a stunning and perfect surprise.

This approach I'm endorsing will net you
A small portion of boundless delight.
Keep believing the world's out to get you.
Now and then you might not be proved right.

II

Something and Nothing

If you had known how little
you would have had to give
to drum into this brittle
hope the desire to live,

would you have changed the venue,
your greeting or your tone
or planned things better when you
knew we'd have hours alone,

and if you heard a hollow
voice spit these ill-advised
questions, would nothing follow?
I wouldn't be surprised.

Telling Strangers

I'm telling strangers how I feel.
I simply blurt it out.
I tell them that my love is real
And pure, and free of doubt.

Some blush, while others beam with pride.
Yesterday, in the queue
At Sainsbury's, I terrified
A lanky youth or two.

My heart is running wild, I say,
With need I can't conceal.
I find it easy to convey
To strangers how I feel.

I'm sure it can't do any harm.
They're flattered; I've confessed.
They're entertained; I'm spent and calm.
I've got it off my chest.

To you, I'd never dare express
The truth. I care too much.
There's no way round this, not unless
You fail to keep in touch,

Ignore me, join the ranks of men
From whom I am estranged.
I promise I will tell you then.
My feelings won't have changed.

How I Feel Now

Make sure to tell me if you go away.
When your computer lets you down, please say.
Don't make me wonder what you are or aren't.
I think I'd rather ruin things today.

If there's a row that you cannot suspend,
A visit from an old, demanding friend,
Warn me ahead of time, and if you can't
I would prefer to call today the end.

The distance I can handle. I can cope
With obstacles, changed plans and shattered hope,
Not silence, though, no matter what the cause.
I think I'd have to opt to cut the rope,

Plummet and smash. At least I'd know what's what.
This fathoming what is and what is not
Crept, wrapped in thrills and danger, through my doors.
And if I need to I will wreck the lot,

Vandalise, batter, desecrate and maul,
And stand and weep, watching the tower fall.
When my most timid wish is quite extinct
I will not be in any doubt at all.

Bedridden, under rubble, trapped in snow –
I will not care. I won't desire to know.
How I feel now, and that our lives were linked
Will be small certainties from long ago.

Living Without You

At the moment I still prefer you
To the poems I've written about you.
I expect this won't always be true.
At the moment I still prefer you
As I wait at the back of your queue
(Trying hard to despise you and doubt you)
For the moment when I'll prefer you
In old poems, and living without you.

From a Stranger

If I took all your words addressed to me
(apart from on that night and in that place)
and forwarded the lot to somebody
with the same name, and watched that person's face
as she surveyed your letters, I would see
no furrows of bewilderment, no blush
acknowledging a bond held privately.
She might think someone who was in no rush
to meet her filled a dawdling gap between
feeding the kids and emptying the bin
with written small-talk that would be obscene
in its omissions if the writer's skin
had once touched hers, once avidly conspired.
But from a stranger, no more is required.

Exorcise

I tried to cry you out of me.
Tears only bred more tears.
I tried to sing you out of me
With songs that worked for years.
I tried to think you out of me
With clean, transparent thoughts.
I tried to scare you out of me
With factual reports,
To bribe you out with images
Of five-star beach resorts.

I tried to write you out of me.
Notice I'm trying still.
I tried to cheat you out of me
By tearing up the bill.
I tried to shame you out of me
By doubling what I owed.
Trying to move you out of me,
I shook your fixed abode.
I tried to pant you out of me
By pounding down the road.

To lock you out, to mock you out
I ridiculed your ways.
I tried to doubt you out of me
By finding lies in praise.
I tried to quote you out of me,
Repeating lines to friends.
I tried to warn you out of me
By fearing tragic ends,
To hoard you out with love that earns
More than it ever spends.

I tried to yawn you out of me
And bored myself to tears.
I tried to wait you out of me
But couldn't spare the years,
Tried to begrudge you out of me
By taking back my dreams,
Then, to betray you out of me,
I cheered for rival teams.
I tried not trying and I failed
Here as in all my schemes.

Friday 13th February 2004

I hope you had bad luck today
In keeping with the date:
You broke down on the motorway
In rain, and had to wait

For hours, and then the shops were closed
Or all the cards sold out.
The valentine you were supposed
To buy, you left without.

If you persisted, went as far
As Open Later stores,
Garages, or the all-night Spar
In your alleged good cause,

I hope you had your wallet nicked,
Were hurled into a van
By coppers eager to convict
A random, blameless man,

And if you made a card, I hope
It fell into the fire.
She'll be annoyed, and you can't cope
With being called a liar.

Don't push your luck. I will concede
That you are hers, not mine.
Since she has you, why does she need
A big fat Valentine?

I hope the envelope explodes,
Gets eaten by the cat.
I bet you're writing 'Love you loads' –
Bad luck, my friend, with that.

The Onus

I will not mention seeing you again
Nor will I cut our time together short,
Tell you my honest view of you, or men,
Reduce our possibilities to sport.
I will be neither saboteur nor life support.

I will spread space around my words and smiles
For you to ask how far is my hotel,
For affirmations, let-downs or denials.
You'll have to be the one to crack the spell.
I will not let you push me and pretend I fell.

Praise you deserve, that I would love to give,
I will withhold, but neither will I rail
Against your house rules or the way you live –
A libertine one day, a man in jail
The next. I won't determine if we thrive or fail.

You'll have to work out what I mean to say,
What I have meant to you. I'll try to be
Neutral in an alluring sort of way.
Onus, a word you'll never hear from me.
(Four letters, burden of responsibility.)

Manifest

Shouldn't the heart aspire to be
a working meritocracy?

You, for example, have the nerve
to snatch more love than you deserve.

Shouldn't I have your lazy smile
crushed at the bottom of the pile?

Shouldn't you rip my rival's coat,
right through the buttons, from the throat?

This is the best that we can do,
and what's impossible for you

and unattainable for me,
we can't ask of society.

Imaginary Friend

I have done everything so far.
I've even told myself you care
until I don't. The lion's share,
the graft, the craft, the whole affair,
travelling miles to where you are.

You have suggested student bars
and endless drinks with friends of yours,
communal curries, walking tours,
oblivious to the pain you cause.
Airless, abandoned things in jars

that cry and crave the light of day
will start reminding me of me
unless some swift emergency
action is taken. I am free
to pop my lid and walk away

into the new. It won't be hard
and when at last you can afford
the time to savour your reward,
climb down to where you left me, stored –
you'll find that I got past the guard.

Drop all your projects and attend
to this alone. Know I returned
only to measure what you'd learned.
You never dreamed you would be spurned
by your imaginary friend.

My Ideal Man

This is what happens, nine times out of ten.
I nurtured fantasy, neglected fact.
I fell in love with an idea again.

I think I might prefer ideas to men.
My dreams had all the qualities you lacked.
This is what happens, nine times out of ten:

I meet a man I hardly know and then
I improvise his words, how he'll react.
I fall in love with an idea again,

In safety, in my mind's protected den.
Then truth intrudes, with neither charm nor tact.
This is what happens nine times out of ten.

You were the perfect notion once, since when
Your real-world counterpart has stalled and slacked.
I fell in love with an idea again,

One I invented with my heart and pen
Who wasn't you. Grand romances contract.
This is what happens, nine times out of ten.
I fell in love with an idea again.

Send

E-mail your lover one full-stop
To let him know he's got the chop,
The old heave-ho, the push, the sack.
Period. Tiny, plump and black,
And if a question mark comes back,

Rows of full-stops across his screen
Will point out starkly what you mean:
You loved him once. Now you do not.
If he mistakes an awful lot
Of full-stops for a dot dot dot,

Go bold, pump up the font, press hash
(The one he made of things), then dash.
For each new season's thriving crop
Of travesties, each wound, each flop,
E-mail your lover one full-stop.

III

The Cutting Dead

My love survived my thinking you were cruel,
That, knowingly, you set out to destroy
My peace of mind. I might have been a fool
For a sadistic thug or bully boy.
My love survived my thinking that your wrath
Was just the darker flip-side of your charm.
No woman wants a man whose heart is froth
You could have done me many kinds of harm
By working on your image as a hulk:
Direct, aggressive, quick to punch and shout.
Instead, the cutting dead, the structured sulk,
The girlish, 'Don't you know? Well, work it out.'
Eureka: you're a man-sized whingeing brat.
Not even love like mine could live through that.

White Feathers

You can blame me for congestion on the London Underground.
You can blame me for the threat the euro poses to the pound,
For the war, for the extinction of Tyrannosaurus Rex –
I will always think that you are scared of sex.

You can misconstrue my jokes, or claim you gave me up for Lent.
You can say the rot set in when I revealed the true extent
Of my appetite for gossip by discussing Posh and Becks –
I will always think that you are scared of sex.

You can try to prove I'm arrogant and cocky and controlling.
You can fume because I never once suggested ten-pin bowling.
You can show me painted enemies with ropes around their necks –
I will always think that you are scared of sex,

Which is why you smashed my heart up. So be in or out of touch;
I've escaped your jurisdiction. I already know too much.
Send me tulips, send me Anthrax, court injunctions, big fat cheques –
I will always think that you are scared of sex.

Yes, unless, until, you change your ways (to, say, Toulouse-Lautrec's)
I will always think that you are scared of sex.

Peace Offering

I believe there are some people
With so little self-respect,
Such a lack of self-esteem that they
Are driven to reject

Anyone who treats them kindly.
If you're nice to them, you're toast,
And the fools who fall in love with them
Are those they hate the most,

But if loving you is really
What you're punishing me for,
Now that I no longer need, desire
Or like you, now I'm sure

You're the rudest, most uptight, disloyal
And ludicrous of men,
Do you think that we might find our way
To being friends again?

In the Chill

I wore no coat. My legs were bare.
I would not feel or see
The greyer nights, the cooler air.
Now it blows into me,

This autumn you concealed so well.
You told me it was spring
And made the swish of leaves that fell
Sound like awakening.

I was the fool in shorts and shades
Cloud-bathing in the chill.
I had been warned that summer fades
But spring meant I could still

Hope for the heat and light to start.
You were my longest day.
Your ice preserves my summer heart
Now winter's on the way.

After the Axe

We're only safe – our homes, our hearts, our friends –
if we confine to distant, lawless lands
the lives of strangers meeting brutal ends.
        You said I had nice hands.

I knew it wasn't true, but didn't mind;
that small white lie that stands out in a swarm
of truth, without which truth is ill-defined.
        Exceptions fix the norm.

My eyes so clear, my mind so sharp, my skin
like artists' paper, forty pounds a sheet –
All these I deemed well worth believing in;
     accurate, therefore sweet.

You dried up, loveless as a Tudor king.
No compliment could be allowed to live
after I wrote that one unwelcome thing,
     and while I can forgive

my skin, so smooth it let you slide away,
my mind, so sharp it sliced you into strands,
my eyes, for witnessing our quick decay,
     I can't forgive my hands.

The Way It Has to Be

Ignoring you at Christmas –
It shouldn't be too hard:
Not buying you a present,
Not sending you a card.

Ignoring you near tinsel
And baubles and mince pies.
Ignoring you while Santa
And Rudolf cross the skies.

Ignoring you at Christmas –
It's absolutely fine.
I've had eight months to practise –
Easy as mulling wine.

Ignoring you with snowmen
And robins on the lawn.
So what if it's the day when
The son of God was born?

Does that make you less heartless?
Does that make you less cruel?
Ignoring you at Christmas.
Ignoring you for Yule.

Ignoring you at Christmas –
The way it has to be.
Not picturing you brooding
By a sparkly silver tree.

Ignoring you at Christmas –
The reasoning is sound.
My head persuades my heart that
It must be all year round,

This silent night we've started,
Which means no Christmas kiss,
No sending love, peace, blessings.
Least of all sending this.

Nothing to Hide

I was thinking of suggesting
that we work together on a full account.
I could contribute words, details, sentences, stories,
poems, an impressive degree of accuracy
about how I felt, behaved, and why.
I could sing all the relevant songs in the relevant rooms.
As a gesture of goodwill I could throw in
some intelligent guesses about why you did what you did.

You could contribute sighs, silences, inert regret,
the image of a lonely mountain topped with snow,
inconsistency, ants in the wilderness, flat boggy land,
platitudes murmured portentously: one of those things,
incompatible lives, too alike, not alike enough.

Once we were both happy with the finished product
(which we never would be – you would never approve my version
and I'd find yours too hazy, impossible to insert
into anything fit for presentation to the public),
I could take half and distribute it all over the world.
You could take half and bury it under your lawn.

What a great collaboration it would be.
I'll give you a ring. I'll give you nothing to hide.

Let's Put the Past in Front of Us

Finally we agree. We share a vision.
Allow me to set out in black and white
Our firm, unspoken policy decision.
Feel free to change the parts that don't sound right.

Let's never meet or talk or make things better.
Let's not consider how we each are flawed.
Let's slam down phones and tear up every letter,
And build a silence that could bend a sword.

Let's trample on our friendship, our potential.
Let's blame each other, bitterly, for years.
Let's call our good times false, inconsequential
And frame in gold the doubts, the threats, the tears.

Let's shred our morals, lock away our manners.
Let's cut our feelings off to spite our hearts.
Let's host a carnival of hate, wave banners,
Parade our grudges through the streets, on carts.

Let's not, while we are younger, braver, stronger
Than we will be again, fight hard to save
Lost hope. Whichever one of us lives longer
Can wail 'Too late' beside the other's grave.

If this is not our dream, our aspiration,
Plan A, hooray, what we would both prefer,
Then, in the name of grief and isolation,
Let us at least behave as if it were.

The Barring Arm

I stare out days and cling to compliments,
wait for it not to matter anymore
that you hold dear your version of events,
assuming that you do; I can't be sure.

It isn't true to say we do no harm
to one another. Silence raises pain
higher than words. It is the barring arm.
Nothing will happen overnight but rain.

Tomorrow I will find I care as much
and am as powerless to put things right
as we are both afraid to be in touch
and waiting. Nothing happens overnight.

Homewrecker

Get in the car.

No one wants to hear what you knew
before they knew it. When asked by the press to comment
upon your dismembering neighbour, do not say
I always suspected he'd do exactly this.

The guru on the ferry gave his word:
Nobody's getting away with anything.
Let him convince you. Do not ask
how, precisely, one goes about becoming a guru.

Drive indirectly home.
Remember, you are afraid of turning left.
Drive indirectly home. Now you are lost, bereft,

and you deserve his love, which you will get.
You're all set to have the wrong children –
too quiet, too well-behaved.
Plenty of time to live by the church and say
*My husband used to be a homewrecker, but now
he is a husband.*

Don't Say I Said

Next time you speak to you-know-who
I've got a message for him.
Tell him that I have lost a stone
Since the last time I saw him.
Tell him that I've got three new books
Coming out soon, but play it
Cool, make it sound spontaneous.
Don't say I said to say it.

He might ask if I've mentioned him.
Say I have once, in passing.
Memorise everything he says
And, no, it won't be grassing
When you repeat his words to me –
It's the only way to play it.
Tell him I'm toned and tanned and fine.
Don't say I said to say it.

Say that serenity and grace
Have taken root inside me.
My top-note is frivolity
But beneath, dark passions guide me.
Tell him I'm radiant and replete
And add that every day it
Seems I am harder to resist.
Don't say I said to say it.

Tell him that all my ancient faults
Have been eradicated.
I do not carp or analyse
As I might have when we dated.
Say I'm not bossy any more
Or, better still, convey it
Subtly, but get the point across.
Don't say I said to say it.

Rubbish at Adultery

Must I give up another night
To hear you whinge and whine
About how terribly grim you feel
And what a dreadful swine
You are? You say you'll never leave
Your wife and children. Fine;

When have I ever asked you to?
I'd settle for a kiss.
Couldn't you, for an hour or so,
Just leave them out of *this*?
A rare ten minutes off from guilty
Diatribes – what bliss.

Yes, I'm aware you're sensitive:
A tortured, wounded soul.
I'm after passion, thrills and fun.
You say fun takes its toll,
So what are we doing here? I fear
We've lost our common goal.

You're rubbish at adultery.
I think you ought to quit.
Trouble is, at fidelity
You're also slightly shit.
Choose one and do it properly
You stupid, stupid git.

Anyone Can Draw a Line

The day that I got over you
The sun was gold, the sky was blue.
I changed at Sheffield, went by train.
What fate, or sense, had tried in vain
To say so many times before
I heard at last. At last I saw.

What sense, or fate, had tried to say
Was that a stunning summer's day
And all life's other little treats –
Kir Royales, sports cars (leather seats) –
Could never be enhanced by you.
You are not good. You are not true.

You are not brave. You are not sound.
Outside the pub, I looked around.
Your absence gave the village scene
That perfect glow. It might have been
Paradise, or the South of France.
For giving you a second chance

Fate could have scolded me with sleet,
Dark grumbling skies. Instead, a treat
Your joyless hand could not describe.
No chance. This shining day's a bribe
I'm way past ready to accept.
Briefly I missed your rude, inept,

Changeable, narcissistic form.
Then I cheered up. It was so warm,
The sun so bright, the sky so clear
The day I made you disappear:
Today, the twenty-eighth of June.
Have a nice life and afternoon.

Progress

The first time you abandoned me
I turned my heart into a vault
For your harsh words. It had to be
A tragic waste and all my fault.

The second time I thought, instead,
Of all the games I wouldn't miss
And laughed all night, in a new bed;
I'm bored – thank God – of you, and this.

Limited

*after being commissioned by O$_2$ to write a Valentine text-message poem
of no more than 160 characters*

Blank spaces count as characters. It's true.
I wasn't sure. And then I thought of you.

A Note on the Text

The pamphlet *Early Bird Blues* was published in 1993 by Smith/ Doorstop Books, and *Second Helping of Your Heart* was published in 1994 by Crabflower Pamphlets. Poems from these two pamphlets that were subsequently included in *The Hero and the Girl Next Door* have been placed in that section in this *Collected Poems*, and are therefore not included in the pamphlet sections. The following poems were originally published in *Early Bird Blues*: 'Categories', 'The End of Love', 'Poem for a Valentine Card', and 'Wrong Again' (under the title 'I Did The Right Thing Once'). The following poems were originally published in *Second Helping of Your Heart*: 'A Soul', 'When I Am Famous', 'Your Street Again', and 'The Philanderer's Ansaphone Message'.

Acknowledgements

'If You Were Standing Where His Shadow Fell' was commissioned for and first published in *Thirteen Poems of Revenge* (Candlestick Press). Some of the other new poems were first published in *PN Review*. 'Unbalanced' was first published in the *The Fountain*, the quarterly magazine of Trinity College, Cambridge

Index of Titles

Index of First Lines